WAY OF THE
TRADER

Every owner of a physical copy of this edition of

WAY OF THE TRADER

can download the eBook for free direct from us at Harriman House, in a DRM-free format that can be read on any eReader, tablet or smartphone.

Simply head to:

ebooks.harriman-house.com/ wayofthetrader

to get your copy now.

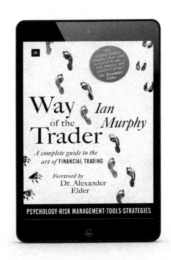

WAY OF THE
TRADER

*A complete guide to the art
of financial trading*

IAN MURPHY

 Harriman House

HARRIMAN HOUSE LTD

18 College Street

Petersfield

Hampshire

GU31 4AD

GREAT BRITAIN

Tel: +44 (0)1730 233870

Email: enquiries@harriman-house.com

Website: www.harriman-house.com

First published in Great Britain and the United States of America in 2019.
Copyright © Ian Murphy.

The right of Ian Murphy to be identified as the Author has been asserted in accordance with the Copyright, Design and Patents Act 1988.

Hardcover ISBN: 978-0-85719-698-9
eBook ISBN: 978-0-85719-699-6

British Library Cataloguing in Publication Data
A CIP catalogue record for this book can be obtained from the British Library.

Charts created using TradeStation. © TradeStation Technologies, Inc. All rights reserved. No investment or trading advice, recommendation or opinions are being given or intended.

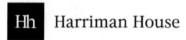 Harriman House

CONTENTS

THE FOREWORD

by Dr. Alexander Elder

THIS IS THE liveliest book on trading I've read in several decades.

Successful trading is partly a science and partly an art. Most writers forget the art part and sink in the sandpit of dry formulas. If formulas alone could make you rich, the firm with the fastest computer and the best programmers would own the exchange. That has not happened because the art part trips them up.

The market is not a physical object that can be mastered with precise formulas. It is a huge mass of people, subject to the imperfect laws of mass psychology. Crowds sweep most of us up, including seemingly rational analysts. And not only that – your feelings, desires and fears color your vision and interfere with your perceptions of the market's reality.

This book by Ian Murphy delivers its share of formulas, but what makes it unique is the amount of attention it pays to the human condition of a trader. It brings you face to face with feelings that spring up in the markets – and suggests solutions.

Most financial traders lose money – it is a sad if seldom discussed fact. The crowds garner some paper profits during a bull market, only to give back much more when that market turns. Trading is a minus-sum game in which the losses of the majority flow into the pockets of a savvy and disciplined minority, after a hefty deduction to the professionals in and around the market. If you trade 'like everybody else' you will lose. To win you have to stand apart, be different.

This is why many successful traders could be described as eccentric. Ian brings his own share of eccentricity to the market – so much so that when he first told me he was writing a book I suggested *The Leprechaun Trader* as its title. Later the conservative minds at the publishing house came up with *Way of the Trader* – true if less colorful.

Ian is a master of the skillful turn of phrase. "People who are drawn to the markets tend to be tech savvy and many have a background in business and finance – what a pity." "It's important we lose money when we start trading." Reading that brought back a memory of how I had the bad luck to make money on my first two trades. Afterwards it took me a couple of years to get rid of the delusion that trading was easy.

Ian continues: "A bad trader is like a bad negotiator, every time he sits down at the table he gets a worse deal." "…the only way to get ahead in the market (to triumph over ourselves), is to act in a manner that is out of character for traders…" "Discipline is not about suppressing or controlling something, it's about doing the appropriate thing at a given point in time."

Ian's book is not all art; there is plenty of science. He delivers well-organized advice on market analysis, indicators, and trading systems. For the past several years Ian has been an active member of SpikeTrade.com – a worldwide group of traders that I lead together with my friend and partner Kerry Lovvorn. Ian credits both of us for many of his tools and rules. I will not hold it against him that he skips a few credits – after reading our posts for years, our concepts must have gotten so deeply under his skin that they feel like his own.

Still, Ian has a uniquely engaging way of presenting those concepts. For example, I've been saying to traders for years that the single most important step for their growth is keeping good records – show me a trader with good records, and I'll show you a good trader. Ian writes: "Slippery people avoid written records like the plague. They try to conduct all their business face to face and never document anything because they know they might have to deny it later. When traders fail to keep proper records, the only person they're hoodwinking is themselves." And he follows this up with a list of seven recommended records.

In a saturated field of market literature Ian's book is like a breath of fresh air: real, humane, and genuinely funny. You'll enjoy reading it, and I hope it helps you become a better trader.

Dr. Alexander Elder
Author, *The New Trading for a Living*

THE
INTRODUCTION

L IFE CONSTANTLY PROVIDES wonderful opportunities. If the opportunity you seek is financial, the markets are the place to be. Every trading day, trillions of dollars flow through the global financial system and, if you are prepared to take a calculated risk, some of it can be yours.

A private trader is someone who uses their own money to trade the markets. There is no other activity like it. Trading offers the unique ability to make serious amounts of cash from anywhere on the globe with just a laptop for company – and, best of all, it's totally legal.

Not surprisingly, the promise of wealth and freedom has attracted many to trading over the years and continues to draw in new traders. As we all know, there is no such thing as a free lunch, not to mention a free buffet. In fact, most people who attend a 'free lunch' in the markets end up having to pay for broken dishes.

Sources of revenue that require no physical effort are quickly identified and soon become saturated. Trading is particularly difficult because the markets are populated by some of the brightest minds on the planet. I have been fortunate to meet some of them and can assure you they were up early this morning and know exactly what they are doing.

In many respects, a trader is like a stand-up comedian. Both professions make their living by observing society and leveraging its anomalies. More importantly, both activities revolve around a single issue. The comedian is either funny or not; everything else is irrelevant. A trader can either pull money out of the market or not; nothing else matters.

In order to do that consistently, training is required and that's where this book comes in. There are three parts:

- **Part A** will take an honest look at the job of a trader and explore a trader's relationship with the market.

- **Part B** has ten sections. These provide a complete foundation for traders, including a look at various trading styles and the path a trader must follow in order to be successful, followed by an 'edge' and how to use it. While each is a complete lesson in its own right, there is a natural progression to these ten chapters and it's assumed readers have already dabbled in the markets. Accordingly, some chapters will demonstrate how risk management and record-keeping deal with the issue of gambling, while others identify the procedures used by professionals. Along the way, there will also be an introduction to technical and fundamental analysis.

- Finally, in **Part C**, I'll share some profitable trading strategies which can be used by anyone.

New traders share a common fault: they over-complicate trading by submerging themselves in technical indicators. Successful trading boils down to just a handful of basic things and for the most part they're not technical in nature. The psychology of trading is especially important. Hence, the style of the book is pithy and personal with as little financial jargon as possible. It's also quirky and unexpected because that's how the market operates. But don't let the light-hearted anecdotes fool you – everything you need to prosper as a trader can be found in the pages that follow.

I've done my best to write it all down, the question is – can you pick it up?

PART

A

THE JOB

Is Trading a Job or a Business?

I N THIS OPENING chapter, we'll look closely at the activity of a private trader and examine aspects of the profession which may surprise people thinking of getting involved.

Working in paradise

About 30 years ago, I decided to move to the Canary Islands. I had been there for brief holidays and concluded the sunny beaches offered better prospects than a floppy-disc factory in Limerick. When I got there, things weren't as rosy as I had imagined and after spending a few weeks handing out fliers for pubs and clubs, I got a job on a construction site.

This involved carrying floor tiles up 20 flights of stairs in the heat of summer. After six months, the building was finally complete and we had a bit of a celebration to mark the event. That evening, as I sat on the rooftop eating a sheep's head with my Moroccan workmates, I couldn't help thinking this was not the high life I had in mind.

Just like an image of a tropical island, working as a trader can look very attractive from a distance. Faraway hills are always greener and may even appear to be made of dollar bills. But trading is a difficult task and is not profitable for the majority of people who attempt it.

There is no shortage of market advisors and we are all familiar with the usual clichés, *'Buy low and sell high'*, *'Cut your losses and let your winners run'* and *'Buy the rumor, sell the news'*. All of these are true but are much easier said than done. Many market advisors are like fringe politicians: they always know what others should be doing but somehow they never manage to be in a position where they have to take financial responsibility for their opinions.

All politics may be local, but all trading is global. When we connect to the market, we plug into an unfiltered display of the financial impact of all human activity and this can come as quite a surprise. Every meeting held, every barrel of oil pumped, every machine sold and every shot fired – they are all distilled to their economic essence and expressed on our screen.

Most of us are unprepared for the enormity and complexity of this experience. Modern society is constantly holding our hand and creating structures designed to protect us from ourselves and others. In a world where uncomfortable truths are avoided for fear of causing offence, the naked directness of the market is shocking.

From the market's perspective, our trading endeavors are just another flow of data to the exchange, feeding into all the other data it receives. It is indifferent to our feelings and opinions and has no understanding of us as a person. All it perceives is a tiny packet of data telling it to execute an order, buried among millions of similar orders.

A business – but a different one

Trading is an exercise in the transference of capital based on the assumption of risk. We might think we are buying and selling shares, but we are actually running a small business which trades in risk.

Therefore, when we start to trade, we need to retire from the concept of doing a week's work for a week's pay and we should dedicate the same level of commitment to our new trading business that we would to any other.

Trading is a little different from other enterprises because we plug in and out of our income source when it suits us. We can trade for a few weeks this year and do nothing for three years, then trade for a solid six months and stop again. In the meantime, we have no customer base to maintain or employees to support.

Another wonderful aspect of trading is the ability to quickly grow an account without having to expand our business to accommodate the increase in turnover. For example, a trader can place a $200 trade or a $2 million trade from the same computer, in the same market. Because of its nature, the market has an infinite ability to assimilate any amount of money thrown at it and give the corresponding return on investment.

If a financial instrument increases in value by 15%, the guy with a $200 trade makes $30 and the guy with $2m in the same instrument makes $300,000 – but no extra effort is required and it all happens in the same place at the same time.

What's more, a trading business never has to chase debtors for payment because all transactions are settled immediately. This is a huge advantage because many start-ups spend half their time running the business and the other half trying to get paid.

And finally, when the day comes that a trader has enough, he can simply stand up and walk away. There is no costly infrastructure to be dismantled or ongoing liabilities to manage.

Cash is king

It goes without saying, we need money to trade and the larger our account, the easier it will be to generate a living wage. Most folks don't have a lump sum to begin with, so they need to save. This will require effort and personal sacrifice. They need to eliminate all unnecessary expenditure and divert every penny to paying off any short-term high-interest loans. This process will also nurture the habits of discipline, patience and diligence which they will need to trade.

Newcomers should start by trading a simulated account of the same size they intend to trade with real money. If they don't manage to get a lump sum together, a steady track record on a simulated account is an excellent calling card if they plan to manage other people's money.

No barriers, no rigging

Professions with high barriers to entry tend to be very profitable and lack competition. On the other hand, professions which are easy to enter pay less and are highly competitive. The trading profession has no barriers, so the profits are elusive and the competition intense.

The market is a work environment like any other. The existing professionals need to get paid and they know where to find the cash. The legal and medical professions aren't rigged against newcomers just because the old hands are plugged into the money flow. When entrants to these professions have naive ideas of making a fortune, disappointment is sure to follow.

Likewise, the trading profession isn't rigged against new traders. The new guys need to appreciate the complexity, composition and subtlety of the environment they have entered. They must learn the ropes and serve an apprenticeship like everyone else before them.

Trading and gambling

My first encounter with financial trading was not a good one. At the time, I was trading precious metals in a workshop which I shared with a goldsmith. One day, our cozy cocoon was ruptured by a group of traders who set up office across the hall.

They were an interesting bunch from very different backgrounds, but all shared the common trait of being a bit odd. In time, I would realize this is not unusual among traders and can actually be an advantage. The most experienced one had worked on a trading floor on Wall Street. He was the group mentor with a great feel for the markets and a sharp mind.

Unfortunately, he was also a bit wired and had a gambling problem. Apparently, his wife had thrown him out and only agreed to take him back if she controlled the family finances. Every morning she gave him £10 for his lunch as he went out to work. He loved betting on the horses, so naturally, the money would be gone before lunch and he would drop into us for a frenzied chat and half my sandwich. As a result, the whole experience left me overwhelmed and undernourished.

Several fascinating studies have been conducted into the behavior of traders and the issue of gambling is a recurring theme. Studies of the market and its participants can be incredibly insightful, especially when conducted by outsiders. Academics approach the subject from a different perspective than the financial industry, so their research offers a valuable counterbalance to established opinion. We traders like to perceive ourselves and the market as two separate entities, whereas an academic sees us as one.

In a 2009 study, Alok Kumar showed a strong connection between the propensity to gamble and investment decisions made by U.S. investors.[1] In the same year, Mark Grinblatt and Matti Keloharju showed that investors prone to sensation-seeking trade more often.[2]

In a very comprehensive study, Brad Barber and Terrance Odean from the University of California and Yi-Tsung Lee and Yu-Jane Liu from Peking University analyzed the complete transaction data for the Taiwan Stock Exchange from 1992 to 2006. They discovered that "the introduction of a National Lottery in Taiwan coincided with a significant drop in trading volume on the Taiwan Stock Exchange."[3]

Many gamblers trade the markets, just as they engage in other activities, but successful traders do not gamble. Understanding the difference goes to the very heart of trading.

A gambler takes on financial risk motivated by addiction and entertainment. The potential for profit is used to justify the activity but he keeps no records, as his losses would destroy the illusion. He bets whenever he has money, regardless of the conditions and potential outcome. He will bet with funds required to maintain his existence, such as food, housing or clothing. If need be, he will forsake these essentials to fund his addiction.

A gambler has wins and losses over time but is always a net loser in the long run.

---

1   Kumar, Alok, 2009, *Who Gambles in the Stock Market*, Journal of Finance, 64, 1889–1933.

2   Grinblatt, Mark, and Matti Keloharju, 2009, *Sensation Seeking, Overconfidence, and Trading Activity*, Journal of Finance, 64, 549–578.

3   Barber, Brad M., Yi-Tsung Lee, Yu-Jane Liu, and Terrance Odean, 2008, *Just How Much Do Individual Investors Lose by Trading?*, Review of Financial Studies.

On the other hand, a successful trader is motivated solely by profit and thinks like an actuary at an insurance company. He examines the market and chooses the risk he is willing to accept, as he knows he is more likely to profit from it than to lose. He constantly limits his risk using proven management techniques and keeps meticulous records. Trading is a regular job to him; he finds it interesting but not particularly exciting. If he believes the current market is not conducive to his trading style, he doesn't trade.

A professional trader also has wins and losses but shows a consistent and steady profit in the long run. Most importantly, he expects a **risk premium**, which means he has to be paid extra for taking the risk: he is not doing it for entertainment.

Honest and accurate records are what separate trading from gambling. The floor of a bookmaker's office is littered with crumpled papers, each one cast aside by an unlucky punter. Every piece of paper is a written record of a financial transaction. This carpet of losses is conveniently trampled underfoot, allowing the customers to ignore the reality of their situation. But the bookmaker doesn't throw away *his* records. That in itself speaks volumes.

Gambling, insurance and trading

The fact that gamblers do not pay a fee to engage with their potential source of profit means the majority of them have to lose in order to support the infrastructure of gambling.

The flow of money in the gambling industry is the exact opposite to the insurance industry. In gambling, the small losses of the many exceed the large wins of the few and the company in the middle pockets the balance. With insurance, the small premiums of the many exceed the large claims of the few and the company in the middle keeps the difference.

A useful exercise for any gambler is to examine the financial statements of a publicly listed bookmaker. For 2017, a global firm reported 'Sportsbook net revenue' of 9.2% across all their platforms and markets. According to their accounts, "Sportsbook net revenue % represents sportsbook revenue expressed as a percentage of sportsbook stakes. Sportsbook revenue is sportsbook stakes less sportsbook customer winnings and the costs for customer promotions and bonuses pertaining to sportsbook."[4] In other words, they keep 9.2% of what they take in.

For a gambler, the bookmaker is the opponent, a more skillful and experienced adversary who sets the odds because he knows he will profit from them over the long run. When you gamble, you play by the bookmaker's rules. When trading, our broker charges us to access the market but he is not our opponent. Our broker is the doorman who must be given a tip as we enter the fray. It's up to us to select the odds we will trade once inside.

In the market, we play by our own rules in an open and transparent public arena. Successful traders have learned how to write their own odds – only then will they pay the doorman.

---

4   Paddy Power Betfair PLC Annual Report and Accounts, 2017.

THE RELATIONSHIP

A Trader and The Market

H AVING LOOKED AT the activity of a trader, we will now examine his place of work, the relationship he has with his employer and other market-related professions.

The market mistress

Trading sounds like the perfect job and it is – provided we have the temperament to survive in the workplace. The renowned English economist John Maynard Keynes described the environment succinctly when he wrote, "The market can stay irrational longer than you can stay solvent." He learned this lesson the hard way when his trading account was wiped out.[1]

---

1   Harrod, Roy, *The Life of John Maynard Keynes*, W. W. Norton & Company, ISBN 978-0393300246.

From the perspective of professional traders, the market is neither rational nor irrational and they avoid the temptation to project their concept of rationality onto it. They see the market as a bipolar empress. She is a trillionaire and it's not their job to correct her or tell her she has no clothes – they let the economists and politicians worry about that.

A trader is the court jester and his job is to hang out with his mistress and benefit from her largesse, while avoiding her wrath. If that involves similar attire, then so be it. This view goes against much of what we have been brought up to believe. Our natural instinct is to try to fix things, to make the situation 'right', because we want things to conform to our concept of normality.

Economic commentators are always complaining about the antics of traders, just as the mandarins of old complained about the jester. When the empress was having a down day, the mandarins would tell her things were not as bad as they looked. On her manic days, they would tell her to relax and take her medicine. But sooner or later, they all ended up in her bad books.

On the other hand, the court jester never offered advice, he just kept on dancing and as a result he never found his head on the block. Likewise, the trick to successful trading is to take the actions of the market with a pinch of salt but our own actions with the utmost seriousness. After all, professional comedy is a very serious business.

Constant rebirth

Not only does the market upset economists, it also defies grammar. The word 'market' is not a noun, it's a verb. And it's not a thing, it's a constantly evolving event. A good gauge of the U.S. market is the S&P 500 Index (the gauge is a bit lopsided because the index is weighted – but that's another story). It was introduced in its current form in

1957 by the U.S.-based financial services company Standard & Poor's. The index is compiled by committee from a selection of 500 large companies trading on the New York and NASDAQ exchanges.[2]

The S&P 500 turns over about 20 firms each year and currently Apple is the largest company in the world by market capitalization, yet the firm is just 42 years old. Alphabet (the parent company of Google) is in second place and is just 20 years old – too young to buy a drink in its home state of California. Facebook, at number eight, has yet to get past the pimple stage.[3]

As younger firms replace older ones and sources of revenue shift online, business owners and managers are scrambling to keep up. New industries and disruptive technologies have had a profound impact on our lives and work environment, yet the market assimilated all of them without missing a single beat. There is nothing irrational about that. The first stock exchange to facilitate continuous trade opened in Amsterdam in 1602 and the market has been 'irrational' ever since.[4] When something has been irrational for that long, it is no longer irrational, but *we* are for thinking it so.

Of course, this is not to say that the markets are always understandable. Just look at human history: if mankind was a person, it would have been committed to a mental health facility long ago. Most of us tend to be reasonable and rational (most of the time), but when we act in groups the intelligence and maturity of our actions sinks to the level of the dumbest person in the room. Considering the markets are driven

---

2   U.S. markets feature prominently throughout this book due to their transparency, liquidity, regulation, ease of access and availability of information. However, the trading tools discussed can be applied to any large international market.

3   *Financial Times* Global 500, 31 December 2017.

4   Lodewijk Petram, *The World's First Stock Exchange*, Columbia University Press, ISBN 978-0231163781.

by mass psychology, we can hardly expect them to be a bastion of enlightenment.

If that feels uncomfortable, let me refer you to Joseph Heller's book, *Catch-22*.[5] When it is put to the hero, "But, Yossarian, suppose everyone felt that way?" He replies, "Then I'd certainly be a damned fool to feel any other way, wouldn't I?"

Trading requires you to adopt the attitude of Yossarian because the market is the ultimate catch-22.

The crisis crew

Market participants are subjected to a constant deluge of seemingly knowledgeable yet often contradictory information. To add to the confusion, respected media outlets run both frivolous and insightful pieces on the same page. Twenty-four-hour financial news channels lean towards the entertainment of observing the markets rather than offering actionable information or analysis.

The language of the market media is also inclined towards the extreme. Markets don't go up, they 'surge' and when going in the opposite direction they 'tumble'. When commentators are personally active in the market (as many are), it adds a tinge of anxiety to their perspective.

One commonly seen headline is, *'Market Makes New All-time High.'* This is diligently reported as some sort of economic accomplishment. It's not. Since their creation, financial markets have always defaulted to new highs. They have to – it's a mathematical guarantee because of inflation. Every day we are alive our age continues to increase, which means our age will 'make a new all-time high' as we take our last breath.

Another classic is, *'Increased Market Uncertainty Due to [insert name of crisis here].'* Certainty doesn't operate on a sliding scale where things

---

5   Heller, Joseph, *Catch-22*, Simon & Schuster, ISBN 978-1451626650.

become more or less certain depending on the circumstances. When you think about it, there is no such thing as certainty and certainly not in the markets.

What we call 'market uncertainty' is the natural order of things, it's when our mistress reasserts her authority and reminds the nanny state who's really in charge of the kids.

My absolute favorite is the word 'as'. It's just two letters long, but what a gem. Let's look at the little guy in action as we consider the following headline: *'Gold Surges as Earnings Disappoint.'* This appears to imply the two events are connected – gold rose because earnings disappointed. However, a few weeks later we see the following headline: *'Gold Climbs as Earnings Outperform.'* This means the complete opposite of the previous headline, but it still makes perfect sense.

This is because the word 'as' can mean *as a result of* but it can also mean *at the same time as*. The word implies a connection but is also valid where none is present. It covers both market directions and all possible outcomes, while still being factually correct each way.

The financial media are not public service broadcasters. They are under no obligation to produce reasoned or balanced articles. They do, however, have an obligation to their shareholders. Financial journalists create a product that sells, and they have been producing it for a very long time.

Strangely, this point eludes many traders in spite of the fact that we have no obligation to reason or balance ourselves. Maybe this explains the contradictory views some of us hold on the media's work. On the one hand, new traders tend to hang on every word written and spoken about the market. Whereas experienced traders go the opposite way and dismiss much of what's written as gossipy and without substance.

Dismal scientists

Economists are another group from whom we expect behavior which is lacking in ourselves. Perhaps this is why we observe their work from polar-opposite positions as well. Market newbies trawl through volumes of economic opinion and analysis, whereas experienced traders tend to disregard the work of many economists as a debate in the university cafeteria. It's all very interesting and intelligent, but completely detached from the 'real world' in the market.

Traders have the wonderful luxury of saying we haven't a clue what's going on and we can take the day off. The technical term for that is 'sitting in cash.' We don't have to explain the market to anyone, least of all ourselves. The market offers endless opportunities and if we don't like the offer on the table today, there will be another one along tomorrow. Our pride and reputation (such as it is), is never at stake because we don't have to make predictions.

Life is not so easy for economists. They must produce information on which planners and decision makers can formulate public policy. When the economists get it right, we're not interested because it's boring and it was obvious anyway. When they get it wrong, we are all experts after the fact and we deride the so-called 'professionals' for failing to predict the future.

Selling the dismal science is not an easy task. The sound and stable policies prescribed by economists are in direct contradiction to what populist politicians and their voters actually want. Jean-Claude Juncker, President of the European Commission, summarized this quintessential dilemma at the height of the eurozone financial 'crisis' when he admitted, "We all know what to do, we just don't know how to get re-elected after we've done it."[6]

---

6 Jean-Claude Juncker, President of the European Commission, in interviews with *Der Spiegel* and the BBC: www.spiegel.de/international/europe/spiegel-interview-with-luxembourg-prime-minister-juncker-a-888021.html; www.bbc.com/news/world-europe-27679170

I don't envy the role of an economist, especially when trying to explain market shenanigans to a concerned public looking for answers. They must feel like a psychiatrist in an arranged marriage with their worst patient and the neighbors keep complaining about the noise.

A trader's perspective

There is no shortage of market commentary. Much of it is well-researched and insightful, and much of it is not. However, commentators perform many different roles, and since they are all getting paid, they must be doing something right – the same can't be said for traders.

We only get paid when we trade successfully. Our opinions are totally meaningless if we can't grow the balance in our trading account. Besides, news events and economic data are not the story we're interested in, we need to know how our mistress – the market – will react. That's a totally different event and the only one that counts.

This gives rise to the market saying, 'It's not the news that matters, but the reaction to it.' The reaction can be in line with the news or run contrary to it. Frequently it does both and in no particular order, so the original story becomes irrelevant. This happens because market-moving events never unfold in a vacuum. Groups of traders always have opposing positions open which are pushing against each other like tectonic plates. These pressure groups (bulls and bears) are constantly trying to drive the market in their direction. This great game in the market never ceases, it merely alters in intensity and location.

An unexpected news event is like an atom bomb dropped on the fault line and it releases the pent-up pressure. When the trading houses start shaking, looters and opportunists jump in and this magnifies the disruption.

In the case of scheduled news events, such as interest-rate decisions or earnings announcements, the market is always front-running the story. Professional traders don't just wait for the news and then place trades accordingly; they also build up positions prior to the event and off-load them into the reaction that follows. This is what 'buy the rumor and sell the news' means and it's why a share price often falls on a good earnings announcement.

In the stock market, for every seller there must be a buyer. Traders selling large positions need lots of buyers to absorb their orders and by selling into a news event they have identified their buyers in advance.

PART

B

A note on the charts

All charts in Way of the Trader *were created using TradeStation 9.5. The original color versions are available at murphytrading.com as well as included in the eBook version, which every purchaser of a physical copy of the book can download for free from ebooks.harriman-house.com/wayofthetrader*

ONE RULE

The Preservation of Capital

N OW WE GET into the practicalities of trading. This first chapter of ten in Part B identifies a trader's most important task: preserving capital.

A study of male and female traders

The majority of traders are men. That is a terrible pity because women tend to fare better when they engage with the market. But don't take my word for it, numerous academic and financial industry studies have confirmed the fact.

As mentioned in the previous chapter, Professor Brad Barber from the Graduate School of Management at the University of California at Davis and Terrance Odean from U.C. Berkeley's Hass School of Business have conducted extensive research and produced a number of studies into the behavior and performance of traders and investors.

One of their most interesting works, 'The Behavior of Individual Investors', was released in 2011 and should be compulsory reading for all aspiring traders. In it they refer to a previous study of theirs which compared the performance of men and women using data from 66,465 trading accounts held at one of the large discount brokers in the U.S. from 1991 to 1996.[1]

They document that "[w]hile both men and women earn poor returns, men perform worse. Virtually all of the gender-based difference in performance can be traced to the fact that men tend to trade more aggressively than women."

In a more recent industry study, one of the largest U.S. brokers – which currently has 26.7 million accounts and processes over 785,000 trades per day – compared the investing behavior of eight million of its retail customers from January 2016 to December 2016. It discovered that accounts held by women outperformed male accounts.[2]

Readers both male and female can probably think of several reasons why this is the case and why women excel at money management. When it comes to spending their own money, women are often masters of self-control with an eye for a bargain. They are also often better organised. Furthermore they are prepared to ask the awkward questions and wait until they get an answer.

Men don't do lists or ask questions. We try to stay in with our 'friends' even after they swindle us and we like to throw our money around to impress people. Like the bull on Wall Street, the market is a triumph of testicular thinking and always has been.

---

1   Barber, Brad M. and Odean, Terrance, *The Behavior of Individual Investors* (7 September 2011). Available at SSRN: ssrn.com/abstract=1872211 or dx.doi. org/10.2139/ssrn.1872211

2   Fidelity Investments, Who's the Better Investor: Men or Women?, 18 May 2017 (www.fidelity.com/about-fidelity/individual-investing/better-investor-men-or-women).
Fidelity by the Numbers: Overview, 31 March 2018 (www.fidelity.com/about-fidelity/fidelity-by-numbers/overview).

Regardless of our gender or character, the market will quickly identify our shortcomings and use them against us to part us from our money. The only way traders can survive in the market environment is to use a set of robust risk management rules and stick to them rigidly, no matter how seductive the market appears.

The one rule of trading, in fact the only rule that matters, is to **preserve capital**. By strictly following this rule, we counter the self-destruction our emotions and wishful thinking inflict on our account. Soon, we will be looking at **the five limits of risk** (page 70) which are practical rules we must apply to our trading in order to preserve our capital.

Conclusion

As we will see in the next chapter, when it comes to investing, a diversified portfolio is essential. Paradoxically, when trading the market, it would appear having both sex chromosomes in the same basket actually yields better results. Perhaps women have a different opinion of the market mistress than men. Whatever the reason, we need to get in touch with the financial aspect of our feminine side and manage our money accordingly.

TWO CHOICES

Keeping it Simple

MOST TRADING DECISIONS involve a choice between just two things. Beginners fail to see the choice as recurring and binary and think it's a unique and multiple choice each time. In the process, they fail to learn from repeated mistakes. Let's take a closer look at some scenarios where traders constantly face two choices.

1. Investing or trading

Small investors buy a stock because they are familiar with the company or read an interesting article about the firm. Managing the position then becomes a pastime. Over the course of the year, they will have wins and losses, and provided they don't do anything too stupid they might even make a few bucks. This type of involvement in the market provides entertainment and distraction with the added possibility of making some profit.

Encouraged by occasional gains, many amateurs believe the way to greater profit is to invest more money over shorter periods. Unwittingly, they have now moved into the realm of trading. Just like a farmer who drives his tractor onto the freeway, that's when the problems begin.

Different games

Baseball and cricket are both played on grass with a bat and ball, but the mindset and culture are completely different. Likewise, investing and trading both occur in the financial markets, but require contrasting approaches. If we are not completely clear which we are doing, we need to stop placing money in the market until we figure it out.

Time frame

Investors and traders are both seeking a return on capital, but their interaction with the market differs in duration and direction. An investment can be held for years, whereas a trade can last just minutes. Investors normally hold long positions, meaning they profit as the price rises. Traders can be long or short at any given time – they are looking to profit on market movement.

A long-term equity investor can enjoy regular dividend payments. A short-term trader doesn't count on dividends and might even have to pay them if he holds a short position on the dividend date. Investors are in it for the long haul and are nearly always invested in something. Traders are just as likely to be sitting in cash, as they wait for the right setup to crystallize.

Once in a position, an investor needs to do very little and is happy to sit back and watch from a leisurely distance. Traders have to be more proactive. They need to be up-close and personal with all their positions – all the time.

Diversification and stability

An experienced investor will have a diversified portfolio spread across multiple asset classes. A trader focuses on just one or two markets and might trade a single instrument repeatedly. Investors seek out emerging trends and, once invested, they hunker down and stay with the position. They like solid companies that do the simple things right. They don't like surprises.

Traders seek out volatility, sharp price reversals and breakouts. Surprise announcements or market pullbacks are manna for traders – quick moves mean quick profits.

Advisors

Investors frequently place money in the markets via an intermediary. Investment advisors have a professional responsibility to their clients, so they will most likely favor a low-risk profile. Traders are their own advisors and have no one to blame when they lose money. They must embrace risk as that is where the profits lie. They need to understand the concept of risk and reward and how this applies numerically to the positions they trade. Every so often, traders must take a hit and be able to absorb it financially and emotionally without a fuss.

One-night trades

Investors usually buy shares directly in a company, a managed fund or an exchange-traded fund (ETF). Traders work with exotic financial instruments, many of which are just a type of contract. An investor seeks out assets which increase in value over time, whereas a trader is looking for anything that moves. In financial terms, investors prefer the security and comfort of marriage, whereas traders do one-night stands. That might sound appealing, but we should remember: surveys consistently show married people are happier and live longer.[1]

---

1   The National Bureau of Economic Research. *How's Life at Home? New Evidence on Marriage and the Set Point for Happiness*, John F. Helliwell and Shawn Grover, December 2014 (www.nber.org/papers/w20794).

Social perception

Somebody who is always engaged in taking risk finds few sympathetic ears when things go wrong. If an investor has a bad year, the markets were not favorable. If a trader has a bad year, he is a gambler and what else did he expect? A trader's 'value' is based purely on his ability to generate profits and there is a view that traders contribute nothing to society.

Investors, regardless of profitability or motivation, are seen as economic stakeholders and necessary for growth. Development agencies and start-ups are always looking for investors, while some governments blame traders for market volatility and use tax structures to discourage 'speculation'.

Tractors are good, sports cars are bad!

Committees

Investing is a slow and steady process which allows time to make decisions and change course. If traders are not happy with a trade, they need to get out quickly and reassess the situation from the sidelines. They don't have time to call a meeting of the investment committee. In fact, traders don't do committees – if anything, they trade against them.

A professional trader will rarely discuss a trade when it's open and will make his decisions in private. Only amateur traders love to talk about their portfolios, almost as if to seek reassurance or validate their decisions. Successful traders say very little and keep their cards close to their chests. Unless you know a trader well and he tells you, you will never know what positions he has open and whether he is ahead of the game or behind.

2. *Lost opportunity or lost capital*

Deciding to make a particular trade or not brings the desire for profit into direct conflict with the fear of loss. If a beginner makes a trade and loses, he gets upset. But if he doesn't make it and it takes off like a rocket – he also gets upset. On closer examination, we see this is really a choice between a loss of opportunity or a loss of capital. We just have to decide which one we are prepared to lose.

They say opportunity knocks only once. That may be true in most walks of life, but trading is not like most other things. One of the marvelous qualities of the market is its ability to provide endless opportunities. A trader will never miss the boat, because the market is a boat builder.

Given the choice between a lost opportunity or losing capital, we need to let the opportunity go. We can't lose something we never had and there will always be more trading opportunities. On the other hand, we might not always have more capital.

3. *Fundamental or technical analysis*

Profitable investing and trading strategies are all based on some form of analysis, of which there are two types: fundamental and technical.

(a) Fundamental analysis

This is an attempt to value an asset by examining its economic and financial attributes. For equities, it involves the financial statements of a firm and their guidance on future earnings. Traders with a background in accounting or economics are drawn to this type of analysis.

Fundamentalists

Long-term investors tend to discount technical signals and rely totally on financial data to inform their decisions. The idea being that common sense will prevail in the long run and fundamentally solid assets will increase in value over time. This is an attractive argument, but not without its problems.

(b) Technical analysis

This involves looking at the historical price action of an asset using charting tools in an attempt to identify recurring patterns. Engineers and those with an interest in computing like the precision and visual signals of this approach.

Technocrats

Short-term traders rely exclusively on technical analysis. Technical purists believe everything one needs to know about a financial instrument is already contained in the price. They believe all market participants (from the highly informed to the totally ignorant) have taken a position based on what they believe will happen next and the result is the current price. Again, there is an attractive logic to this perspective, but it has its limitations.

Irrational people

Assuming an asset will respond in accordance with the underlying financial data is assuming humans will act in a rational manner when facts are presented to them. Unfortunately, humans don't. If they did, all statisticians would love to fly and nobody would smoke.

People act in an irrational and illogical manner all the time. Many highly successful firms make a fortune from illogical and irresponsible behavior because people keep doing things with their money they are not supposed to. In many respects, fundamental analysis is based on trust. We expect investors to do the 'right thing' with their money based on the available information.

Technical analysis has no such trust issues. It's based on what people are actually doing with their money and there is no presumption market participants will eventually do the right thing. Unfortunately, technical types tend to surrender this advantage by thinking on a short-term basis. They know the current price of everything but the long-term value of nothing.

Which type of analysis to use?

Both methods have advantages and disadvantages and should be used in tandem. How much of each to use will depend on our trading style and we will be looking at that in the **Three Styles** chapter.

Regardless of which approach we take, all analysis is pointless unless we can use it to make a profit. For traders, it's never an academic pursuit where the production of reports and data is an end in itself.

4. To use a protective stop or not

After we board a flight, the safety announcement asks us to locate our nearest exit, "Bearing in mind, it might be behind you." When we trade, our nearest exit is always behind us. It's called a **protective stop**.

Also known as a stop-loss order, this is an order sitting on our broker's server which will close our position automatically if the price trades at, or beyond, that level. This is the most important tool in a trader's toolbox and we should always choose to use one.

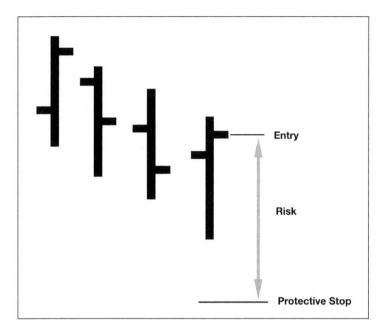

FIGURE 1: THE ENTRY POINT, RISK AND PROTECTIVE STOP ON A TRADE

The function of a protective stop

Apart from closing a losing trade, a protective stop allows a trader to ring-fence his financial exposure. He writes the birth and death certificates of the trade at the same time. The trade is temporary and this is crystallized from the outset.

Traders who see their accounts wiped out by a handful of huge losses share a common trait – they don't use protective stops. This lifesaving tool allows a trader to survive and thrive in a hostile environment. Protective stops are not a standalone feature and are just one element of a trading strategy, so we will be looking at them in more detail in the **Ten Tools** chapter.

5. Whipsaw or lag

This can be the most frustrating choice for some traders and many beginners don't even know they're making it.

(a) Whipsaw

A whipsaw happens when the price hits a protective stop and closes a position, then reverses and starts trading higher, except the trader is no longer in the position. Not only is he out of the trade, but he also missed the opportunity to profit from the rebound. Two losses in one event.

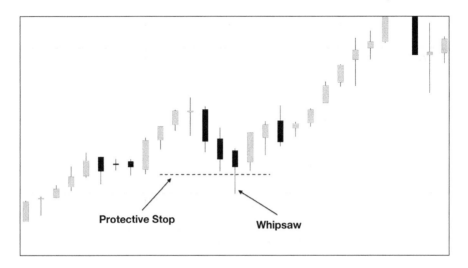

FIGURE 2: CANDLESTICK CHART SHOWING A WHIPSAW WHERE A PROTECTIVE STOP WAS HIT AND THE MARKET REVERSED AND CLIMBED HIGHER

Why do whipsaws happen?

It's incredible, the number of traders who open a position in a popular stock at a breakout level and put a protective stop a few cents under the previous low or a set percentage away from the entry price. You don't have to be a genius to work out where all the stops are sitting.

The market pros watch that level closely and when the market drifts near it again, they act. They throw a sizable order at the price and, like a basketball thrown into a room full of mouse traps, all the orders trigger. Because protective stops are market orders, they execute at any price and there is a race to the bottom.

Once the mayhem is over, there are no sell orders left at the current price level, so the market has no option but to reverse direction. The whipsaw is complete, and the market climbs higher.

When protective stops are triggered, who buys some of the shares being dumped? Perhaps it's the traders who are now riding the stock higher. And perhaps the profit they made is more than the price of a basketball. For this reason, whipsaws are often referred to as a 'fake out' or a 'shake out'.

Living with whipsaws

A whipsaw is never a one-off event. It keeps happening because these reversal points are the market sending out feelers, looking to see if the next step will be up or down.

FIGURE 3: A SERIES OF WHIPSAWS ON A DAILY CHART OF FACEBOOK (NASDAQ: FB) IN 2017

When a trader understands whipsaws in this context, he realizes good trade ideas can still be stopped out. The trader was at the winner's table, but he passed out because his necktie was too tight. He should loosen the stop a little (but not too much) and re-enter the trade if the favorable conditions still exist.

Every job has annoying and repetitive aspects. Trading a whipsaw-dependent strategy is one of the annoying tasks a trader must perform. It's just one of those things – it goes with the job.

Whipsaws also mean a trader has to keep questioning his view on the market. He keeps asking, should he be buying this stock knowing what he knows now? When the market keeps telling him he's wrong, eventually the message sinks in.

(b) Lag

Trading a lag-dependent strategy is where the protective stop is placed deeper down the chart, well outside the incessant gossip and drama of the market – in order to stay in a trade longer.

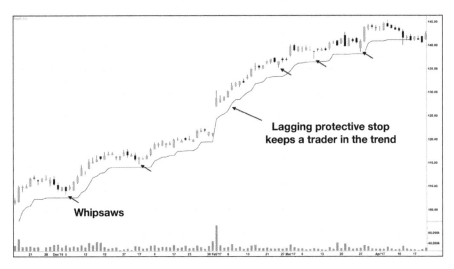

FIGURE 4: DAILY CHART OF APPLE (NASDAQ: AAPL) WITH A LAG-ORIENTATED STOP

Some traders prefer this approach because they've been whipsawed one time too many. Maybe their lifestyle doesn't allow time to get to the screen to re-enter when a stop order triggers and they keep missing the opportunity. But lag is not the perfect solution either, and it's not without some drawbacks.

Living with lag

If a trader's preferred strategy is lag-orientated, he might have to sit through a drawdown of up to 20–30% in a position. This means the trade size will be smaller because he has to reduce the number of shares he buys to accommodate a large pullback without exceeding his risk limit. Of course, the flip side of this means his gains will also be smaller.

If a trader prefers the tight stops of a whipsaw approach, they can hold larger position sizes, but they need to have the time available to re-enter trades. If they are part-time traders, chances are they will get the email to re-enter when it's most inconvenient.

Choosing between whipsaw and lag

There are no perfect solutions in trading, just scenarios which present different challenges and require different management techniques. A trader needs to pick the least worst choice, the one he can live with. Whipsaw requires the discipline of action, whereas lag requires the discipline of patience – neither is perfect.

In the **Three Styles** chapter, we will examine how the whipsaw/lag trade-off relates to different trading styles. In **The Strategies** chapter we will explore whipsaw- and lag-dependent strategies.

6. Shares or something else

This is multiple choice, but it should be a binary decision for beginners. Because the markets are always on the edge of some 'crisis' or another, we should keep the things we trade as simple as possible, and it doesn't get simpler than shares.

(a) Shares

Online trading has introduced a kaleidoscope of trading opportunities and it can be a daunting task for new traders to know where to start. In my opinion, beginners should avoid any financial instrument which has an expiration date and doesn't have an underlying asset.

Trading blue-chip equities on the long side ticks all the boxes for new traders. This is because stock markets default to the upside in the long run and bull markets tend to last longer than bear markets, so the chances of long equity trades working out are higher.

Besides, most people who express an interest in trading have already dabbled with shares. This allows them to concentrate on learning the mechanics of their trading platform, without having to learn a new market as well. Also, the relative stability and security of blue-chip equities affords beginners the luxury of trading slower time frames.

Beginners should also avoid products where losses can exceed deposits, and never trade anything they don't fully understand. If we can't figure out how a financial product works, there is a good chance most other people don't know either. That matters when the market drops and people panic.

Shares trade on highly regulated and transparent exchanges. The regulators get some flack, but they are very active and constantly pursue wayward market participants. When we buy shares, we are buying a piece of a company that actually exists and most of them make real money. That reassuring and simple fact matters when life in the market gets complicated.

(b) Exchange-traded funds (ETFs)

After equities, these are the next logical step. ETFs trade like a stock but contain a basket of assets or track an index, commodity or bond. We should never trade an ETF unless we fully understand what assets it holds. This can be found in the fund's fact sheet, which should be available on the ETF provider's website. When ETFs are geared or 'inverse' (the fund moves in the opposite direction to its underlying assets), we need to know exactly how that is done.

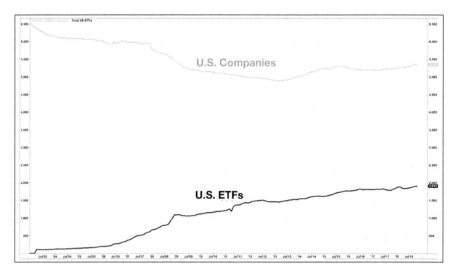

FIGURE 5: THE NUMBER OF U.S.-LISTED FIRMS AND ETFS FROM JANUARY 2003 TO NOVEMBER 2018. FIRMS HAVE DECLINED FROM 6,554 TO 5,350, WHILE ETFS HAVE INCREASED FROM JUST THREE IN 2003 TO 1,912 TODAY

World Federation of Exchanges

ETFs have grown in number and popularity to a point where private traders can trade everything from real estate to volatility in a single inexpensive instrument. Some ETFs have been turbocharged, so every move in the underlying asset is magnified three times in the fund. These triple-X funds can be hair-raising at times but can also be highly profitable if traded correctly.

An interesting experience for any trader is to spend a year in the markets only to discover an index-tracking ETF performed better than they did. This raises the question of why we trade stocks at all. Would it not be better to buy an index-tracking ETF during market pullbacks and do little else?

The answer to that question is… maybe. Like everything else in the market, it's not as simple as it first appears. Shares are like soccer players. An index tracker supports the whole team and averages out the abilities of each player. But a team of dependable Average Joes never win the cup – for that you need good strikers.

Celebrity strikers are moody, overpaid and always surrounded by drama. But they are worth the hassle because every so often they pull off a truly magical shot which saves the game. We trade individual stocks because we are looking for high-profile strikers with the magic touch. They bring serious profit to the beautiful game of trading.

A handful of great trades during the year are what make trading worth the effort. When we least expect it, an individual stock can pull off a magical move and kick our account balance into the sky. The same stock might be held in an index tracker, but the mediocre performers dull the striker's brilliance.

(c) Futures

After stocks and low-risk ETFs, futures should be the next port of call. Futures are a contract for the delivery of a commodity or financial instrument at a set price – in the future. They trade in a similar manner to shares and allow for much higher leverage. Each contract is a set size, so a larger account will be required to trade things like oil where a lot is 1,000 barrels.

In the U.S., smaller lot sizes using 'eMini' contracts are available for indices, commodities and forex. Many successful traders work exclusively with eMinis of the S&P 500 index and trade nothing else. eMinis on the CME exchange offer an almost 24-hour trading window during the week, as they trade from Sunday to Friday 17:00

to 16:00 (CT) with a break from 15:15 to 15:30 and daily maintenance from 16:00 to 17:00.[2]

(d) Forex

Forex or foreign exchange is the largest trading market in the world by volume. According to the Bank for International Settlements, trading regularly averages in excess of $5 trillion per day.[3] Much of these transactions are carried out by institutional traders but there is ample room for the small guy. Forex is a 24-hour market, so the use of risk management is essential.

There have been numerous high-profile cases of manipulation of the forex markets. It's an area of financial trading which looks attractive because you trade a currency pair, one against the other. However, this is one binary choice which can generate a lot of pain for the inexperienced.

A 2014 report by the Autorité des Marchés Financiers (Financial Market Authority) in France, which looked at 14,799 accounts trading CFDs and forex over a four-year period, concluded that 89% of clients lost money.[4] A similar report by the Komisja Nadzoru Finansowego (Financial Supervision Commission) in Poland found 82% of forex traders lost money in 2011.[5] This level of loss is not unique to French and Polish traders.

---

2   CME Group (www.cmegroup.com/trading/why-futures/welcome-to-e-mini-s-and-p-500-futures).

3   Bank for International Settlements, Triennial Central Bank Survey of foreign exchange and OTC derivatives markets in 2016 (www.bis.org/publ/rpfx16).

4   Study of investment performance of individuals trading in CFDs and forex in France (PDF) (www.amf-france.org/technique/multimedia%3FdocId%3Dworkspace%253A%252F%252FSpacesStore%252F9bf2caa8-1ce4-4832-85f4-4dffcace8644%26).

5   Komisja Nadzoru Finansowego (www.knf.gov.pl)

(e) CFDs, binary options and spread betting

Products such as contracts for difference (CFDs) are promoted due to their tax advantages, and providers of binary options highlight the low cost of entry. Financial spread betting blurs the lines between trading and gambling. These types of instruments carry additional risks and are off limits to retail traders in some countries – accordingly, I believe they should be avoided by beginners.

(f) Cryptocurrencies

The inner workings of Bitcoin and other cryptos are a mystery to the majority of us. If cryptos are here to stay, they will be around for a long time and there is no rush to get in on them now. Futures contracts for Bitcoin were only launched in December 2017 and financial regulators are still getting to grips with this new form of finance. The crypto story is only beginning and it's not until the market turns sour on them (which happened almost immediately after the futures were launched), that we'll get an insight to their true value.

THREE STYLES

Trend Following, Swing Trading and Day Trading

ALL TRADING BOILS down to just three styles. In this chapter, we will examine each in turn.

Time frames in the market

Like a dad who can't dance, the market has only three moves: up, down and sideways. Unfortunately, the apparent simplicity of this scenario is complicated by the fact that the market expresses these movements in different time frames. A share that is rising on a daily chart could be falling on a weekly chart, while rising on a monthly chart – all at the same time.

Traditionally, short-term movements in the opposite direction to the prevailing trend are described in terms of an ocean **tide**, with **waves** and **ripples**. The long-term monthly trend is the tide, weekly movements back and forth are the waves and daily volatility are the ripples. Since the stock market keeps going higher with every new tide, we can add the impact of climate change and say the sea level is constantly rising.

Because 'market direction' is based on the snapshot of time we analyze, each time frame should be matched with a particular trading style – of which there are three:

1. *Trend following*

With trend following, we take a position in a stock as it moves in an upward trend. Once in, we stick with the trend until it ends. Also known as **position trading**, the style is really only suited to trading on the long side and works best with large established stocks.

A train journey

Following a trending stock is like taking a train journey. We step on board and join the crowd when the train pulls into our chosen station. We temporarily become part of something which is moving in the direction we want to go, and we get off when the train stops going in our chosen direction. We just don't know when that will be, so we are always standing ready.

One of the most important things to realize about trend following is that we can rarely get in at the very start of a new trend or time our exit to coincide with the top. Our goal is to catch a bit in the middle. Just like a subway train, the majority of passengers don't get on at the first station on the line and get off at the last one. Trying to buy at the bottom and sell at the top of a trend is a common (and expensive) mistake beginners make. If we are trading a trend-following style correctly, we will always enter *after* the bottom has been established and exit *after* the trend has topped out.

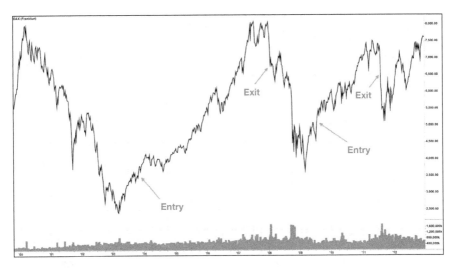

FIGURE 6: TYPICAL ENTRY AND EXIT POINTS WHEN FOLLOWING A TREND
(DAX INDEX, XETRA)

If you think about it, the bottom is only apparent after the trend has already changed to the upside. So we have to wait for it to actually manifest on the chart – and by then it's over. Likewise, the top can only be seen in the rearview mirror on the way down. We should forget about jumping the gun and trying to catch tops and bottoms of trends as they are forming.

Attempting to predict the bottom and catch the trend reversal will just see us catching the proverbial 'falling knife' and buying into a loss. Likewise, attempting to sell as the trend tops out will see us getting out on a small pullback and missing the rest of the trend. We never know how far the trend will go because we only realize the extent of the move after it's over.

Longevity

Trending stocks have two things in common: a good fundamental story, and they keep going for longer than anyone expects. As each new high is taken out and each pullback fails to end the trend, the pundits keep telling us it can't last. But it does. If we catch four or five of these trends a year, while controlling our losses elsewhere, we will be highly profitable traders.

In the previous chapter, we looked at the concept of whipsaw and lag. To fully embrace a trend-following style we must be committed laggards. We must accept that our exit point (protective stop) will often be a long way from the current price. This means we have to sit through many pullbacks in order to give the trend room to breathe as it climbs higher.

(a) Monthly trend following

They say a drummer is someone who hangs out with musicians. I don't know much about that, but a monthly trend follower is an investor who hangs out with traders. In this slow and steady style, each bar (or candle) on our chart represents a full month of trading activity. This form of 'trading' is really technical investing, where we make our entry and exit decisions based on clearly defined signals rather than company financials or macroeconomic events.

The trend is our friend

Institutions and large money managers use the monthly time frame quite a bit. With this style, we must be prepared to sit tight on our stock for years and not be spooked by every bit of negative news. On the other hand, we have to be prepared to drop shares we have owned for ages, without getting attached to them. 'The trend is our friend', but we shouldn't get too clingy.

Trading a monthly chart is a bit like investing in the property market – trend changes are common knowledge by the time they are technically confirmed. For example, when we have been sitting in cash and our indicator signals an entry, the recovery in the stock market might have been in the news for months. Likewise, when we get our sell trigger the market pullback will be well underway and we might be sitting on a sizable drawdown already.

Monthly trend following is incredibly easy to learn and is almost guaranteed to make a profit. But very few of us have the ability to embrace this style because we lack the required discipline and patience. Trading off a monthly chart sounds simple in theory but every price bar takes a full month to form, so waiting for the last day before taking action can prove impossible.

Dow theory

With monthly trend following we need to be aware of **sector rotation** as profitability passes from one area of the economy to another. Growth and tech stocks are all the rage as a bull market powers ahead, whereas defensive dividend-paying stocks look attractive when things are going south. Practitioners of monthly trend following should also therefore be familiar with *The Dow Theory*,[1] especially the accumulation and distribution phases of the market.

Seeing is acting

Monthly trend following is suitable for long-term accounts, which means practitioners of this style are also DIY fund managers. But that doesn't mean we should manage our pension pot ourselves. It's one thing for loving partners to suffer a lifetime of leaking roofs but managing the family savings is too important to entrust to enthusiastic DIY types.

This is especially relevant because fund managers have an advantage over us. When a few people are monitoring a monthly strategy, they are more likely to act on the signals. They might have a meeting once a month, make a documented decision each time and instruct their

---

1   Dow Theory by Chad Langager and Casey Murphy, Investopedia (www.investopedia.com/university/dowtheory).

trading desk to act accordingly. When we are acting alone and have been looking at the same thing for a long period, frequently we no longer 'see' it.

How many of us have a broken roof slate we have been meaning to fix for the past three years? Do we have a load of junk in the garage we are going to clean out 'soon'? This is a serious problem for monthly trend followers. Worse still, when a trend has been intact for years, we might even stop checking our charts altogether.

It's a good idea to let a friend or fellow trader know if you are trading a monthly strategy. They should know your entry and exit signals well and review them once a month. We might also consider a trading platform which facilitates conditional orders. This allows us to program orders which will trigger at the end of the month if our requirements are met.

Actively passive

Monthly trend following also needs to be considered in terms of the 'passive versus active' debate. Passive investors build a portfolio of assets which match the weighting of a specific index or they simply buy some index-tracking ETFs. After that, they sit back and do very little as they are content to make returns in line with the market's performance. As the name suggests, an active investor is more involved in the process as they weave in and out of positions in an attempt to outperform their passive colleagues and the general market.

Both approaches have advantages and disadvantages. Passive strategies tend to sit through drawdowns when they don't have to and active strategies tend to overtrade and accrue unnecessary charges. The trick is to be passive when the market is trending and active when it's turning. In **Part C**, we will look at a strategy which allows us to do just that.

(b) Weekly trend following

Beginners are surprised to learn that weekly trend following is widely considered to be the most profitable style of trading. Technically it is an easy style to learn, but it can be the most challenging. At least with monthly charts, we can forget about the market for 30 days at a time, but weekly trend following is more demanding.

We need to be prepared to move our protective stops at least every weekend. Depending on our strategy, we might also be monitoring the price action on a daily closing basis. We have to monitor our open positions more closely (but not too closely), which means we will experience more instances where we are tempted to stray from our strategy and intervene.

This style is particularly suited to beginners as they have more action to keep things interesting but need only check open positions on weekends. This allows time to get away from the screen (physically and mentally) and concentrate on their day job. To trade this style, we need to understand the basics of trend structure and have the patience to wait for each weekly bar to slowly print out without jumping in or anticipating where it might go.

Sitting around

Unfortunately, most beginners ignore this very promising style because it doesn't offer the action they expect – it's just too boring. After all, they became traders to trade, not to sit around, right? This is a gross misunderstanding. We become traders to pull money out of the market. If we can do that by waiting around, then that's exactly what we need to do.

One of the most influential trading books ever written is called *Reminiscences of a Stock Operator*. It describes the experiences of Jesse Livermore, one of the world's greatest stock traders. Livermore was a trend follower and he informs us, "It never was my thinking that made the big money for me. It was always my sitting."[2]

2. Daily swing trading

Daily swing trading is probably the most common trading style. In this case, each price bar represents one full day's trading, so each week in the market is five bars on the chart. Depending on our perspective, this offers a fivefold increase in opportunity or brings us five times closer to the fire.

Swing trading is all about identifying the exact moment when the energy in a trade shifts from potential to kinetic and the stock sparkles into life. We are trying to catch a short-term market trend or its reversal, so swing trades can be with the prevailing market trend or against it.

Normally we expect to be in a swing trade for a few days or a week at most. As soon as the short-term move ends, we get out of the position. This type of trade works out quickly or not at all. Once we are in the trade, we only need to adjust our orders after the market closes. If we know how to set up conditional orders, we don't even have to be at the screen to trade. Hence, this style is suitable for part-time traders who want to be more active in the market.

Entries and exits

Good entries and exits take on more importance with this style because the 'swing' might not last very long and profits can be wiped out after a day or two. We also need to move our protective stop to a break-even position as soon as possible, all the while observing the

---

2   Lefèvre, Edwin, *Reminiscences of a Stock Operator*, Harriman House, ISBN-13: 978-0857195944.

whipsaw/lag trade-off. In addition, because things are now happening a lot faster, we have less time to make decisions.

Moving our orders at night as we relax with a beer might sound easy, but we have to adjust them every night without fail. If we share the same time zone as the market we are trading, this should not present a problem. If we are living somewhere else, it means we must adjust orders in the wee small hours of the morning or during our working day.

Again, we are back to the **Two Choices** trade-off. Do we trade at unusual hours to gain access to a more liquid market or do we sacrifice liquidity to trade more sociable hours?

One of the common errors daily swing traders make is to be seduced by the speed of the market and drop down to an intraday time frame to monitor the action more closely. Dissecting the daily bar is never a good idea because the market can go all over the place in a single trading session, but actually go nowhere from a daily perspective.

Weekend warriors

Holding a swing trade position over the weekend is something else we need to consider. A lot can happen between the close on Friday afternoon and the open on Monday morning. If a swing trade gaps down a few per cent at the open, we will often lose more than our allotted risk amount. If the same position was held in a weekly trend-following trade, we would most likely still be in the trade and within our allocated risk. Frequently a pullback which kicks us out of a daily swing trade will be the very trigger to enter a weekly trade.

In the market we should expect the unexpected at all times, and manage our positions accordingly. I rarely hold a full-size swing trade position over the weekend. During the week, I take some profit off the table and move my protective stop to break-even. Frequently, I will close the trade on Friday afternoon rather than risk an unexpected news event over the weekend. Panic tends to be exaggerated on Monday morning, because the panicky types have had two days to wind themselves up.

3. Day trading

When trend following and swing trades are open, managing them requires very little time. It takes no more than ten minutes to log on to our account and adjust protective stops. The rest of the time, we might think we are 'trading' when in fact we're just mindlessly looking at the market moving.

Day trading is very different. When we trade intraday (opening and closing a position in the same session), we have to actively trade all the time and the market will punish us severely if we don't. There is no cut off or break where we can assess the situation calmly and adjust our orders in peace. It's a case of grabbing small profits in the face of large risk, like picking up coins from in front of a steam roller.

If we know what we are doing, we can make serious money very quickly when day trading. We can take on a large position with very low risk if we catch a sharp price reversal at the right time. This magical but dangerous spot, where the risk is lowest and the reward highest, is what traders are always searching for. But day traders need to be able to do quick mathematical calculations and possess ironclad discipline, otherwise they will get themselves into all sorts of trouble.

It's difficult to trade well, but trading well against the clock is something else entirely. All the usual risk management rules apply to day trading, but the process unfolds much faster so we don't have time to think.

Technical indicators are less useful on intraday time frames. All indicators lag to some extent, because they are calculated from a look-back window, but the shorter the time frame we are trading, the more acute the problem becomes. It's like looking in the rearview mirror while weaving through traffic on the freeway. For this reason, day traders place more emphasis on the interpretation of price action alone. Understanding this requires some specialist training and there is also an art to it.

We can set our intraday price bars for any time period of our choosing and there is some debate in the trading community about the issue. One school of thought suggests any time frame shorter than 30 minutes when trading equities produces too much random movement to be tradable. This is called 'market noise' or 'market gossip' because it's loud and constant and prevents us from getting to the facts.

Choosing which intraday time frame to trade is a case of finding the point where we believe the lagging technical facts are starting to outweigh the live market gossip.

The Taiwan and France studies

Many people drift into day trading and try it out for a while to see if they can do it. In 2010 Barber, Lee, Liu, and Odean released another paper based on their analysis of the Taiwan Stock Exchange called, 'Do Day Traders Rationally Learn About Their Ability?'[3]

The conclusion stated:

> "The most experienced day traders lose money and over half of all day trading can be traced to traders with a history of losses. Persistent trading in the face of losses is inconsistent with models of rational learning. So, too, is the decision to try day trading when ex-ante expected lifetime profits are negative. For prospective day traders, 'trading to learn' is no more rational or profitable than playing roulette to learn."

---

3   Barber, Lee, Liu, and Odean, *Do Day Traders Rationally Learn About Their Ability?* (faculty.haas.berkeley.edu/odean/papers/Day%20TradersDay%20Trading%20and%20 Learning%20110217.pdf).

In the French study mentioned previously,[4] the conclusion stated, "… the study also indicates that investors who trade the most (by number of trades, average trade size or cumulative volume) lose the most."

When we are getting burned we need to move away from the fire, not closer. Shortening the time frame we trade is not the solution to losses, it exacerbates them. We should go in the opposite direction and trade on charts with longer time frames. In other fields of activity, intense immersion in a subject yields better results, in the market it is counterproductive.

For all the reasons mentioned above, I don't believe day trading is suitable for beginners. From my own experience and from speaking to people who coach traders, I can confirm that day traders are the ones with most of the problems – mental, emotional and financial.

Conclusion

For many people 'financial trading' is synonymous with day trading. But the activity of trading actually covers a very broad spectrum. Beginners should start out by trading equities on a longer time frame and progress to shorter ones as their experience and knowledge grows. Eventually they will settle on a style and market which suits them. Often this happens only after they have traded a time frame or instrument beyond their comfort zone and decide to take a step back from the fire.

They shouldn't allow others to influence this process because each trader comes to the game with different skills. Experienced traders concentrate on their preferred style and fine-tune strategies to trade it successfully. Over time, this can lead to an 'I did it my way' attitude

---

4   Study of investment performance of individuals trading in CFDs and forex in France (www.amf-france.org).

as a professional's focus narrows and they believe their style is the best. In the process, they might discount styles more suited to others. Beginners should keep an open mind and try out all the styles.

FOUR LEGS

The Attributes Which Support a Successful Trader

R EASON, RISK, RESPONSIBILITY and routine are the four legs under a trader's desk – without them, our account will come crashing to the floor.

1. Reason

At all times, we need to apply reason and logic to trading. How we deal with our thoughts and emotions is what makes or breaks a trader. Financial trading is not for the faint-hearted, but neither is it for the brave-hearted. In fact, the less heart we have the more likely our trading will be successful.

On the other hand, we should not be too intellectual, because we cannot out-think the market. Bringing an intelligent and well-educated mind into the market is like driving an oil truck into a river. Something which was previously an asset suddenly becomes a liability.

If you are unfortunate enough to be burdened with above average intelligence, you need to dumb it down, because you will keep finding complicated solutions to simple problems.

People who are drawn to the markets tend to be tech savvy and many have a background in business and finance – what a pity. Unfortunately for them, financial trading is not about finance or trade, it's about thoughts and emotions. Accordingly, new traders come to grips with the technology quickly, but continue to struggle with their mind and heart for years.

On the other hand, artistic types rarely trade the markets – another pity. An artist's ability to identify structure and mood in a nebulous environment is exactly the skill needed to thrive in the financial markets. And this is one of the many paradoxes of trading; people drawn to the process are often ill-equipped and the best suited are not interested.

The well-known market analyst Robert R. Prechter graduated from Yale University with a degree in psychology and after a four-year stint as a professional musician he joined Merrill Lynch as a market technician. He tells us, "After I decided to make markets a career, I realized that mass psychology is what they're all about."[1]

Mark Douglas, an experienced futures trader, identifies and addresses the many psychological challenges traders face in his excellent book, *The Disciplined Trader*. In the preface he tells us:

> "As a trader, you have the power either to give yourself money or to give your money to other traders. And the ways in which you choose to do this will be determined by a number of psychological factors that have little or nothing to do with the markets."[2]

---

1   Prechter, Robert Rougelot, *Prechter's Perspective*, New Classics Library, 1996, ISBN 0932750400, 9780932750402.

2   Douglas, Mark, *The Disciplined Trader: Developing Winning Attitudes*, New York Institute of Finance, ISBN-13: 978-0132157575.

Timothy Slater developed the first software program to plot commodity graphs and technical indicators on personal computers. Mr. Slater wrote a foreword to Mark Douglas's book, where he tells us, "I sincerely feel that success in trading is 80 percent psychological and 20 percent one's methodology, be it fundamental or technical."

Head office

The professional and personal experience of all these people is telling us the same thing – successful trading takes place in our head office. The application of reason rather than emotion or sentiment is the key.

Having a detached, logical and methodical approach to our trading is not about suppressing or denying our feelings. That's never a good idea. Rather, we need to accept we will have strong emotional responses to the market and see these emotions as part of the job without over indulging them. Over time, as we learn to invest less expectation and fear into each individual trade, our emotional reaction to the outcome will diminish accordingly.

Adios ego

When we have a strong attachment to notions of 'me, myself and mine', the process becomes 'my gain, my loss, my orders, my account, my trading, my money... my life!' The solution to this is to get 'me' out of the way and just trade. This doesn't mean we don't exist when we trade successfully – of course we do. The problem is ego. That is what needs to be sidelined.

Market don

Obsession with ourselves inevitably gives rise to the concept of the 'other'. In the market environment, this can manifest as an imaginary foe in the form of institutions and their 'smart money'. We become a modern-day Don Quixote, jousting with the giant glass skyscrapers on Wall Street, believing them to be a threat. To make matters worse, because they are a fabrication of our imagination, these towering glass mirrors reflect and magnify our fears and will always be our arch nemeses.

Temporary mutual interest

Not only have we to remove 'me' from the market, we also have to remove ourselves from the crowd. Successful traders think and act as individuals. Collective decision making, consensus and collaboration are all very well for the board of our local golf club, but groupthink is highly destructive in the market environment.

When the majority of people believe strongly in a market direction, that is the point where the market begins to reverse. When everyone rushes to one side of the see-saw because it's going up, their collective weight pushes it back down again. This crowd mentality lulls traders into a false sense of security as they believe there is safety in numbers.

When the market is trending strongly, this is certainly the case, but it also means traders are part of a bigger target when the mood reverses. The key is to go with the crowd when it suits you and leave when it doesn't. A trader's involvement with market trends should be based on temporary mutual interest, not loyalty.

Mental viscosity

Ultimately, the fluidity of our mind will determine our success in the market. Those of us with solid and stodgy views on how things should operate will struggle when trading. Whereas traders with a flowing and flexible outlook will easily adapt to everything the market throws at them.

Because psychology and the application of reason is so important to trading, we will continue to explore this theme. Also, in the **Six Edges** chapter, we will examine the most appropriate psychological tools to apply to trading. But don't let that put you off – we won't be studying Freudian theory. It will be simple 'common sense in common use'.

2. Risk

The United States and the United Kingdom have prospered because of their entrepreneurial spirit and willingness to embrace risk. Over the centuries, daring men and women took to the seas, risking their money and their lives – and those risks paid off. Just as the daring sea captains of old faced uncharted tides in pursuit of fortunes, traders must face the uncharted markets which abound with opportunities and dangers.

Underwriting risky ventures

Before we throw caution to the wind and set sail, we should remember the escapades of these early swashbucklers were subject to 'terms and conditions'. Their high-seas ventures would not have been possible without the support of insurance companies whose appetite for risk was more reasoned. Insurance firms are generally not perceived as being risk takers, if anything the opposite – but that's exactly what they are.

The top ten global insurance brokers (by revenue) are based in the U.K. and the U.S., as are the most influential global stock exchanges.[3] In these two countries, the mindset for taking risks and managing them properly endures to this day. They understand that without risk there will be no reward – but the risk must be calculated and controlled.

Professional risk takers

Just like underwriters, traders must put their necks on the line, all the time. Traders have to be professional risk takers, because that's where the rewards lie. They have to have the confidence and courage to take the steps others dread. They have to navigate the stormy seas others fear. In simple terms – they just have to go for it!

---

3   Insurance Information Institute, *International Insurance Fact Book 2017*, p.12 (www.iii.org).

If we have an aversion to risk, we will have an aversion to trading. Each time we trade, we will either gain or lose something, and how we relate to this recurring process will determine our success. The key to embracing risk is to understand it and become familiar with it. We do this by assessing and managing it. Every day before we trade, we should conduct a thorough risk assessment where we identify the current risk, quantify the potential loss and put measures in place to manage it.

Risk assessment and management

I used to manage an office of insurance loss assessors. We negotiated claims on everything from fires and floods to accidental damage and financial loss. We saw firsthand how individuals and firms would take out insurance in the hope of never needing it and suddenly find themselves standing in a pile of ashes, anxiously clutching a charred policy document.

Within a few minutes of arriving at the scene, we would know if the policy holder had conducted proper risk assessments and introduced procedures to mitigate against potential losses. The assessment of risk is not very exciting and tends to be avoided by most of us. But trust me when I tell you, assessing the risk before the event is less painful than assessing the loss afterwards.

When we trade, our risk assessment should be no different from any other business. As private traders we are extremely lucky, because the risk and exposure is very easy to quantify and manage. We also have the added bonus that our loss will never be anything more than financial. To conduct our risk assessment, we just need a calculator and a basic understanding of the laws of probability.

Probability versus prediction

We all seek security and certainty in our lives, and in an attempt to get them we instinctively form views and opinions on the future. Traders bring this bad habit into the market. Rather than attempting to predict the future, we should realize only one of three things can happen: the market can go up, down or sideways. As soon as we expect one of these to happen, we are excluding two other possibilities and have reduced our chance of success by 66.6%.

We have no control over the market, but we have total control over our response to it. Instead of forming a fixed view on the future, we should prepare plans for the three possible outcomes. And when the market does move, we need to implement the plan appropriate to that direction – even when we believe the market is going the 'wrong way.' The market never goes the wrong way – we do.

The law of large numbers

First identified in 1713 by Jacob Bernoulli, the law of large numbers states that the long-term results from a set of repeated actions will eventually default to average. However, it's the 'relative frequency' of the results which evens out in the end, not individual results. It's each result divided by the total number of results – which means clusters of similar results and anomalies will occur throughout the process.

Kerrich's coin-flip experiment

In 1940, the English mathematician John Kerrich was visiting his in-laws in Denmark when the Germans invaded, and he spent the rest of the war in a prison camp. He passed the time by conducting experiments on probability and the law of large numbers with another inmate, Eric Christensen. In one well-documented test, they flipped a coin 10,000 times and recorded the results, which Kerrich later published in *An Experimental Introduction to the Theory of Probability*.[4]

---

4   Kerrich J.E., *An Experimental Introduction to the Theory of Probability*, E. Munksgaard (1946) ASIN: B0006AS3No.

Table 1.

2000 successive spins of an ordinary coin.

0 denotes tail.

1 denotes head.

```
          0 0 0 1 1 1 0 1 0 0 1 1 1 1 1 0 1 0 0 0 1 1 0 1 0 1 1 1 1 0 0 0 1 0 0 1 1 0 0 1 0 0 0 0 0 1 1 1 0
          0 0 1 0 1 0 1 0 1 0 0 1 0 0 0 0 1 0 0 1 1 0 0 0 1 0 0 0 0 1 1 1 0 1 0 1 0 0 0 1 0 0 0 0 1 0 1 1 0 1
          0 1 1 1 0 1 0 0 0 0 1 1 0 1 0 0 1 0 1 0 0 0 0 0 1 1 1 1 1 0 1 1 1 1 1 0 0 1 1 0 1 1 0 0 1 0 1 0 1 1
          0 1 0 1 0 0 0 0 0 1 1 0 0 0 1 1 1 0 0 1 1 1 1 1 0 1 1 0 1 0 1 0 1 1 0 1 0 0 1 1 0 1 1 0 1 1 0 1 1 0
          0 1 1 1 1 1 0 0 0 0 1 1 1 0 1 1 0 0 0 1 0 1 0 0 1 0 0 0 0 0 0 1 0 1 0 0 1 1 1 1 1 1 1 0 1 1 1 0 1 0 1 1
          1 0 0 0 1 1 0 0 0 1 1 0 0 0 1 1 0 0 0 1 1 0 0 1 1 0 1 0 0 1 0 0 0 0 1 0 0 0 0 1 1 1 0 1 1 1 1 0 0 0
Row 7>    1 1 1 1 1 1 1 0 0 0 0 0 0 0 0 0  1 1 0 1 0 1 1 0 1 0 0 1 1 1 1 1 0 1 1 1 0 0 1 0 0 1 0 1 0 1 1 0 0
          1 1 1 0 1 1 0 1 1 1 0 0 1 0 0 0 0 0 0 1 0 0 0 1 1 0 0 1 0 1 1 1 1 1 0 1 0 0 1 1 1 1 0 0 0 1 0
          0 0 0 0 1 0 0 1 1 0 1 0 1 1 1 0 1 0 1 0 1 1 0 0 1 1 1 1 1 0 1 1 0 0 1 0 0 0 0 0 1 1 0 1 0 1 1 1 1 1
          1 1 0 1 0 0 0 1 1 1 1 1 1 0 0 1 0 1 1 1 1 1 1 0 0 1 1 1 0 0 1 1 1 1 1 1 1 0 1 0 0 0 0 1 0 0 0 0 0
          0 0 0 0 1 1 1 1 1 0 0 1 0 1 0 1 0 1 1 1 0 0 0 0 1 1 0 1 1 0 0 1 0 0 0 1 0 1 0 0 0 0 1 1 1 1
          1 1 0 0 0 1 0 1 0 0 1 1 1 1 1 1 1 0 1 1 0 1 1 1 0 1 0 1 1 1 0 1 1 0 1 0 0 1 0 1 1 0 1 1 0 0 1 1
          0 1 0 1 0 0 1 1 0 1 1 1 1 1 1 1 0 0 1 0 1 1 1 0 0 0 0 1 1 1 0 1 1 1 1 1 1 0 0 0 0 0 1 0 0 1 0 0 1
          0 1 0 0 1 1 1 0 1 1 0 1 1 0 1 1 0 1 1 0 1 1 1 1 1 1 0 0 0 0 0 1 0 1 0 1 0 1 0 1 0 1 0 1 0 0 1 0 0 1
          1 1 1 0 1 1 0 1 1 1 0 0 1 1 1 0 0 0 0 0 0 0 1 0 0 1 1 0 1 0 1 0 0 1 1 0 0 1 0 0 0 0 1 0 0 1 0 0 1 1 0 0
          1 0 1 1 1 1 0 0 0 1 0 0 1 1 0 1 0 1 1 0 1 1 0 1 1 1 0 0 1 1 0 1 0 0 1 0 1 0 1 0 0 0 0 0 0 0 1 0 0 0 0
          0 0 0 0 1 0 1 1 0 0 1 1 0 1 0 1 1 0 1 1 1 1 1 1 0 0 0 1 0 1 1 0 0 1 0 0 0 0 1 1 1 0 0 1 1 0 0 1 1
          1 1 1 0 0 1 0 1 0 1 1 0 1 0 0 0 0 0 1 1 0 0 0 1 0 0 1 1 0 0 0 1 0 0 1 0 0 0 1 1 0 0 1 0 0 0 0 1 0 0 1
          0 1 0 0 0 0 1 1 1 0 0 0 0 0 0 1 1 1 0 1 1 0 1 1 1 1 0 0 1 1 0 0 1 1 0 1 0 1 0 1 0 1 1 0 1 0 0 1 0 1 1
          0 1 0 0 0 0 0 1 1 1 0 1 1 0 1 0 0 0 1 0 0 0 1 1 1 0 0 1 0 0 0 1 1 1 0 0 0 0 1 0 1 0 0 0 0 0 0 0 1 0
          1 0 0 1 0 0 0 1 0 1 1 0 0 0 0 1 0 0 1 0 1 0 0 0 1 1 1 1 1 1 0 1 1 0 1 1 1 1 0 1 0 1 0 1 0 1 0 0 0 0
Row 22>   0 1 1 0 0 0 1 0 1  0 0 0 0 0 1 0 0 0 0 0 0 0 0 0 0 1 0 0 0 0 0 0  1 1 0 0 1 0 0 0 1 1 0 1 1 1 0 1 0 1 0
          1 1 0 1 1 0 0 0 1 1 0 1 1 1 0 1 0 1 1 0 0 1 0 0 1 0 1 1 1 0 0 0 1 0 1 1 0 1 1 0 1 0 1 0 1 0 1 1 0 1 1 0
          0 0 0 0 1 0 1 1 0 1 1 0 1 1 0 1 0 1 0 1 0 1 0 0 0 0 1 1 1 0 0 1 1 1 0 0 0 1 1 0 1 0 0 1 1 1 0 1 1 1 0 1
          1 0 0 0 1 1 0 1 1 1 0 0 0 0 0 1 0 0 1 0 0 1 1 1 1 0 0 0 0 0 1 0 1 0 0 0 0 0 1 0 1 0 0 0 0 1 1 1 1 0 1 0 0
Row 26>   0 0 1 1 1 1 1 1 1 1 1 1 1 1 1 1 0  1 0 1 0 1 0 0 1 0 0 1 1 0 0 0 1 0 1 1 1 1 0 0 1 0 1 0 1 0 0 0 1 1 1 1
          1 1 0 0 0 1 1 0 1 0 1 0 1 0 0 1 1 0 1 0 0 1 0 1 1 1 1 1 0 0 0 0 1 1 0 1 1 1 1 0 1 1 0 0 1 0 0 1
          1 1 1 1 1 0 1 0 0 0 0 0 1 1 1 0 1 0 1 0 1 1 1 1 0 1 0 1 0 1 1 1 0 0 0 0 0 1 0 0 0 1 0 1 1 0 1 0 0
          1 0 0 1 1 0 1 0 0 0 0 1 0 1 1 1 1 1 0 1 1 1 1 0 1 0 1 1 0 0 1 1 0 1 0 1 1 1 1 0 0 0 0 0 1 0 1 1 0 0 1 0
          0 0 1 1 0 1 1 0 1 0 1 1 1 1 1 1 0 1 0 1 1 1 0 0 1 0 0 1 0 0 1 1 0 1 1 0 0 0 0 1 0 0 0 1 0 0 0 1 0 0 0
          0 1 0 1 0 0 1 1 0 0 0 1 1 0 1 0 0 1 1 1 0 1 0 0 0 0 0 1 1 0 0 1 1 0 0 0 1 1 1 0 1 0 1 1 1 1 0 0 0 1
          1 1 0 1 0 1 1 1 0 1 1 1 0 1 0 1 1 0 1 1 0 1 1 1 0 0 1 1 1 1 0 1 1 1 0 0 1 0 1 0 1 0 1 1 0 1 0 0 0 0
          0 1 0 1 1 1 1 0 1 0 0 1 1 1 0 1 1 0 0 1 0 0 1 1 1 0 0 0 1 1 1 0 1 1 0 0 0 0 1 1 1 0 0 1 1 1 1 1
          0 1 1 0 1 0 1 1 1 0 1 1 1 0 0 1 1 0 1 1 0 0 0 1 1 0 0 1 1 1 0 0 1 0 1 1 1 0 1 0 1 0 0 1 0 0 1 0
          1 0 1 0 0 0 1 1 0 1 0 1 1 1 0 1 1 0 0 0 1 1 1 1 1 0 0 0 0 0 1 1 0 0 0 0 0 0 0 1 0 0 1 1 1 0 1 0 1 1
          1 0 0 0 1 0 1 1 1 1 0 1 0 0 0 1 0 1 1 1 1 1 1 0 1 1 0 1 0 0 0 0 1 1 1 1 1 1 1 0 1 1 0 0 0 0 0 0 0 1 0
          1 0 1 1 1 1 1 1 0 1 1 1 0 0 0 1 0 0 0 0 1 1 0 0 0 0 1 1 1 1 1 1 0 1 0 1 0 0 1 1 1 0 0 0 0 0
          0 0 0 0 1 1 1 1 0 1 1 1 0 0 0 1 1 1 0 1 0 1 0 0 0 1 0 1 1 0 0 0 1 1 0 1 1 1 0 1 0 0 0 1 1 1 0 1 1 1
          1 0 0 0 0 0 1 0 0 0 0 1 1 0 1 0 0 0 0 0 0 1 0 1 0 0 0 0 1 0 1 0 1 0 0 0 1 0 1 1 0 0 0 1 0 1 1 1 1 0 0
          0 0 1 0 1 1 1 0 0 1 0 1 1 1 0 1 0 0 1 0 1 1 0 0 1 0 1 1 0 1 0 0 0 1 1 0 0 0 0 1 1 1 0 0 0 0 1 1 1
```

FIGURE 7: RESULTS OF THE FIRST 2,000 COIN FLIPS FROM THE KERRICH EXPERIMENT

Each coin flip had a possible 50/50 outcome, but heads came up 50.67% of the time. According to the Law of Large Numbers, heads will default to 50% the longer the experiment continued. A closer look at the data reveals it's not uncommon to get eight or nine heads or tails in sequence.

In row seven (marked with the chevron) there are seven heads followed by nine tails. In row 22, there are five tails, followed by a head, followed by nine tails, then another head, but six tails followed. That's 20 tails out of 22 flips! In row 26, there are 12 heads in sequence. Yet, in theory, every flip of the coin had a 50/50 possible outcome.

The gambler's fallacy

The notion that a recurring sequence of one result will be balanced out immediately after by the opposite result is known as the 'gambler's fallacy'. Experiments like the coin flipping by Kerrich disprove the idea. For example, row seven appears to confirm the fallacy, where seven heads are followed by nine tails, whereas rows 22 and 26 prove the notion to be false and the results are random.

The trader's approach

The law of large numbers, Kerrich's experiment and the gambler's fallacy are important to traders because they show three facets of probability in action:

(a) Because we trade for short periods, the law of large numbers may not apply.

(b) Every trade we take is totally random and has no connection to the previous occurrence.

(c) Clusters of similar results occur at random.

Traders with a background in math love crunching the probability numbers, but that's one rabbit hole to be avoided. For Kerrich, a 50/50 outcome was inevitable over time because the coin was indifferent to the outcome and was subject to the laws of physics. The forces which drive the market ignore the laws of physics – and every other law too!

Whenever I think of Kerrich and his coin experiment, I can't help wondering why he decided to go to Denmark in the middle of a war when the place was about to be invaded by the enemy. Had he not calculated the probability of being imprisoned? Traders must work with numbers, but we must also be acutely aware of the economic and political world around us.

Therefore, traders have to utilize risk management tools which can simultaneously address short-term mathematical anomalies, long-term trends and unexpected events. Thankfully, experienced traders discovered how to perform this difficult task and developed a set of rules based on their experiences. The rules work by controlling our exposure to risk in five ways.

The five limits of risk

(a) THE 1% LIMIT

The total amount of money placed in a trade must be less than 1% of the daily turnover of a stock. This ensures we only trade position sizes which are liquid relative to a stock's trading history.

Liquidity is a measure of the price and volume of a stock. Low-volume penny stocks are to be avoided, high-volume blue-chip names are the way to go. The higher the price and the greater the volume, the easier it is to get in and out of a position without affecting the price. This is especially important when we are trading a large account or using long-term trading styles.

A stock trading at $6 with an average daily volume (over three months) of 300,000 would churn $1.8m worth of shares on average per day. If our total position size in a trade is $20,000, this would exceed 1% of the daily turnover ($18,000), so we should not trade that stock. A stock trading at $15 with a volume of 625,000 would turnover $9.375m worth of shares per day. 1% of that is $93,750 – so it's OK to trade.

A simpler option is to have a fixed level of liquidity and avoid everything else. For example, we might set a minimum price of $8 per share and a minimum volume of 400,000 and ignore anything below those levels. We will be taking a closer look at liquidity in the **Nine Filters** chapter.

(b) THE 2% LIMIT

One of the core concepts of risk management in trading is to risk a small fixed amount each time. This can be challenging to embrace because we want to put more money into a trade that looks very good and less money into one which looks a bit flaky. It is only when we carry out a year-end analysis of our account that we realize why this approach is profitable.

Nobody knows what will happen next in the markets. When we place a trade, we are paying for the answer. Regardless of how much we risk, the answer will be the same. Therefore, we need to establish a limit on how much we are prepared to pay for market answers.

Something often bandied around is that we should risk no more than 1–5% of our account on any single trade. A novice trader searching the internet for advice on risk management is likely to find this range crop up repeatedly. Like so much information on the web, these figures bring more confusion than clarity. There is a significant difference between 1% and 5% and the spread is magnified when we have a string of losses. For example, if we are trading a $100,000 account and have five losses in a row, 1% risk on the reducing balance will leave us $4,901 out of pocket, whereas 5% risk will see us down $22,621 and change.

Trade	0.5% Risk			0.75% Risk			1% Risk			1.5% Risk			2% Risk			3% Risk			4% Risk			5% Risk		
	Open $	Loss $	Close $	Open $	Loss $	Close $	Open $	Loss $	Close $	Open $	Loss $	Close $	Open $	Loss $	Close $	Open $	Loss $	Close $	Open $	Loss $	Close $	Open $	Loss $	Close $
1	100,000.00	500.00	99,500.00	100,000.00	750.00	99,250.00	100,000.00	1,000.00	99,000.00	100,000.00	1,500.00	98,500.00	100,000.00	2,000.00	98,000.00	100,000.00	3,000.00	97,000.00	100,000.00	4,000.00	96,000.00	100,000.00	5,000.00	95,000.00
2	99,500.00	497.50	99,002.50	99,250.00	744.38	98,505.63	99,000.00	990.00	98,010.00	98,500.00	1,477.50	97,022.50	98,000.00	1,960.00	96,040.00	97,000.00	2,910.00	94,090.00	96,000.00	3,840.00	92,160.00	95,000.00	4,750.00	90,250.00
3	99,002.50	495.01	98,507.49	98,505.63	738.79	97,766.83	98,010.00	980.10	97,029.90	97,022.50	1,455.34	95,567.16	96,040.00	1,920.80	94,119.20	94,090.00	2,822.70	91,267.30	92,160.00	3,686.40	88,473.60	90,250.00	4,512.50	85,737.50
4	98,507.49	492.54	98,014.95	97,766.83	733.25	97,033.58	97,029.90	970.30	96,059.60	95,567.16	1,433.51	94,133.66	94,119.20	1,882.38	92,236.82	91,267.30	2,738.02	88,529.28	88,473.60	3,538.94	84,934.66	85,737.50	4,286.88	81,450.63
5	98,014.95	490.07	97,524.88	97,033.58	727.75	96,305.83	96,059.60	960.60	95,099.00	94,133.66	1,412.00	92,721.65	92,236.82	1,844.74	90,392.08	88,529.28	2,655.88	85,873.40	84,934.66	3,397.39	81,537.27	81,450.63	4,072.53	77,378.09
6	97,524.88	487.62	97,037.25	96,305.83	722.29	95,583.54	95,099.00	950.99	94,148.01	92,721.65	1,390.82	91,330.83	90,392.08	1,807.84	88,584.24	85,873.40	2,576.20	83,297.20	81,537.27	3,261.49	78,275.78	77,378.09	3,868.90	73,509.19
7	97,037.25	485.19	96,552.06	95,583.54	716.88	94,866.66	94,148.01	941.48	93,206.53	91,330.83	1,369.96	89,960.86	88,584.24	1,771.68	86,812.55	83,297.20	2,498.92	80,798.28	78,275.78	3,131.03	75,144.75	73,509.19	3,675.46	69,833.73
8	96,552.06	482.76	96,069.30	94,866.66	711.50	94,155.16	93,206.53	932.07	92,274.47	89,960.86	1,349.41	88,611.45	86,812.55	1,736.25	85,076.30	80,798.28	2,423.95	78,374.34	75,144.75	3,005.79	72,138.96	69,833.73	3,491.69	66,342.04
9	96,069.30	480.35	95,588.96	94,155.16	706.16	93,449.00	92,274.47	922.74	91,351.72	88,611.45	1,329.17	87,282.28	85,076.30	1,701.53	83,374.78	78,374.34	2,351.23	76,023.11	72,138.96	2,885.56	69,253.40	66,342.04	3,317.10	63,024.94
10	95,588.96	477.94	95,111.01	93,449.00	700.87	92,748.13	91,351.72	913.52	90,438.21	87,282.28	1,309.23	85,973.04	83,374.78	1,667.50	81,707.28	76,023.11	2,280.69	73,742.41	69,253.40	2,770.14	66,483.26	63,024.94	3,151.25	59,873.69
11	95,111.01	475.56	94,635.46	92,748.13	695.61	92,052.52	90,438.21	904.38	89,533.83	85,973.04	1,289.60	84,683.45	81,707.28	1,634.15	80,073.14	73,742.41	2,212.27	71,530.14	66,483.26	2,659.33	63,823.93	59,873.69	2,993.68	56,880.01
12	94,635.46	473.18	94,162.28	92,052.52	690.39	91,362.12	89,533.83	895.34	88,638.49	84,683.45	1,270.25	83,413.20	80,073.14	1,601.46	78,471.67	71,530.14	2,145.90	69,384.24	63,823.93	2,552.96	61,270.98	56,880.01	2,844.00	54,036.01
13	94,162.28	470.81	93,691.47	91,362.12	685.22	90,676.91	88,638.49	886.38	87,752.10	83,413.20	1,251.20	82,162.00	78,471.67	1,569.43	76,902.24	69,384.24	2,081.53	67,302.71	61,270.98	2,450.84	58,820.14	54,036.01	2,701.80	51,334.21
14	93,691.47	468.46	93,223.01	90,676.91	680.08	89,996.83	87,752.10	877.52	86,874.58	82,162.00	1,232.43	80,929.57	76,902.24	1,538.04	75,364.19	67,302.71	2,019.08	65,283.63	58,820.14	2,352.81	56,467.33	51,334.21	2,566.71	48,767.50
15	93,223.01	466.12	92,756.90	89,996.83	674.98	89,321.85	86,874.58	868.75	86,005.84	80,929.57	1,213.94	79,715.63	75,364.19	1,507.28	73,856.91	65,283.63	1,958.51	63,325.12	56,467.33	2,258.69	54,208.64	48,767.50	2,438.37	46,329.12
16	92,756.90	463.78	92,293.11	89,321.85	669.91	88,651.94	86,005.84	860.06	85,145.78	79,715.63	1,195.73	78,519.89	73,856.91	1,477.14	72,379.77	63,325.12	1,899.75	61,425.37	54,208.64	2,168.35	52,040.29	46,329.12	2,316.46	44,012.67
17	92,293.11	461.47	91,831.65	88,651.94	664.89	87,987.05	85,145.78	851.46	84,294.32	78,519.89	1,177.80	77,342.09	72,379.77	1,447.60	70,932.18	61,425.37	1,842.76	59,582.60	52,040.29	2,081.61	49,958.68	44,012.67	2,200.63	41,812.03
18	91,831.65	459.16	91,372.49	87,987.05	659.90	87,327.15	84,294.32	842.94	83,451.38	77,342.09	1,160.13	76,181.96	70,932.18	1,418.64	69,513.53	59,582.60	1,787.48	57,795.13	49,958.68	1,998.35	47,960.33	41,812.03	2,090.60	39,721.43
19	91,372.49	456.86	90,915.63	87,327.15	654.95	86,672.19	83,451.38	834.51	82,616.86	76,181.96	1,142.73	75,039.23	69,513.53	1,390.27	68,123.26	57,795.13	1,733.85	56,061.27	47,960.33	1,918.41	46,041.92	39,721.43	1,986.07	37,735.36
20	90,915.63	454.58	90,461.05	86,672.19	650.04	86,022.15	82,616.86	826.17	81,790.69	75,039.23	1,125.59	73,913.64	68,123.26	1,362.47	66,760.80	56,061.27	1,681.84	54,379.43	46,041.92	1,841.68	44,200.24	37,735.36	1,886.77	35,848.59
21	90,461.05	452.31	90,008.74	86,022.15	645.17	85,376.99	81,790.69	817.91	80,972.79	73,913.64	1,108.70	72,804.94	66,760.80	1,335.22	65,425.58	54,379.43	1,631.38	52,748.05	44,200.24	1,768.01	42,432.23	35,848.59	1,792.43	34,056.16
22	90,008.74	450.04	89,558.70	85,376.99	640.33	84,736.66	80,972.79	809.73	80,163.06	72,804.94	1,092.07	71,712.86	65,425.58	1,308.51	64,117.07	52,748.05	1,582.44	51,165.61	42,432.23	1,697.29	40,734.94	34,056.16	1,702.81	32,353.35
23	89,558.70	447.79	89,110.91	84,736.66	635.52	84,101.13	80,163.06	801.63	79,361.43	71,712.86	1,075.69	70,637.17	64,117.07	1,282.34	62,834.73	51,165.61	1,534.97	49,630.64	40,734.94	1,629.40	39,105.55	32,353.35	1,617.67	30,735.69
24	89,110.91	445.55	88,665.35	84,101.13	630.76	83,470.38	79,361.43	793.61	78,567.81	70,637.17	1,059.56	69,577.61	62,834.73	1,256.69	61,578.03	49,630.64	1,488.92	48,141.72	39,105.55	1,564.22	37,541.32	30,735.69	1,536.78	29,198.90
25	88,665.35	443.33	88,222.02	83,470.38	626.03	82,844.35	78,567.81	785.68	77,782.14	69,577.61	1,043.66	68,533.95	61,578.03	1,231.56	60,346.47	48,141.72	1,444.25	46,697.47	37,541.32	1,501.65	36,039.67	29,198.90	1,459.95	27,738.96
26	88,222.02	441.11	87,780.91	82,844.35	621.33	82,223.02	77,782.14	777.82	77,004.31	68,533.95	1,028.01	67,505.94	60,346.47	1,206.93	59,139.54	46,697.47	1,400.92	45,296.55	36,039.67	1,441.59	34,598.08	27,738.96	1,386.95	26,352.01
27	87,780.91	438.90	87,342.01	82,223.02	616.67	81,606.34	77,004.31	770.04	76,234.27	67,505.94	1,012.59	66,493.35	59,139.54	1,182.79	57,956.75	45,296.55	1,358.90	43,937.65	34,598.08	1,383.92	33,214.16	26,352.01	1,317.60	25,034.41
28	87,342.01	436.71	86,905.30	81,606.34	612.05	80,994.30	76,234.27	762.34	75,471.93	66,493.35	997.40	65,495.95	57,956.75	1,159.14	56,797.62	43,937.65	1,318.13	42,619.52	33,214.16	1,328.57	31,885.59	25,034.41	1,251.72	23,782.69
29	86,905.30	434.53	86,470.77	80,994.30	607.46	80,386.84	75,471.93	754.72	74,717.21	65,495.95	982.44	64,513.51	56,797.62	1,135.95	55,661.67	42,619.52	1,278.59	41,340.93	31,885.59	1,275.42	30,610.17	23,782.69	1,189.13	22,593.55
30	86,470.77	432.35	86,038.42	80,386.84	602.90	79,783.94	74,717.21	747.17	73,970.04	64,513.51	967.70	63,545.81	55,661.67	1,113.23	54,548.43	41,340.93	1,240.23	40,100.71	30,610.17	1,224.41	29,385.76	22,593.55	1,129.68	21,463.88
31	86,038.42	430.19	85,608.23	79,783.94	598.38	79,185.56	73,970.04	739.70	73,230.34	63,545.81	953.19	62,592.62	54,548.43	1,090.97	53,457.46	40,100.71	1,203.02	38,897.69	29,385.76	1,175.43	28,210.33	21,463.88	1,073.19	20,390.68

Half the account is gone

72

Trade	3% Risk Open $	3% Risk Loss $	3% Risk Close $	4% Risk Open $	4% Risk Loss $	4% Risk Close $	5% Risk Open $	5% Risk Loss $	5% Risk Close $	6% Risk Open $	6% Risk Loss $	6% Risk Close $	7% Risk Open $	7% Risk Loss $	7% Risk Close $	8% Risk Open $	8% Risk Loss $	8% Risk Close $	9% Risk Open $	9% Risk Loss $	9% Risk Close $	10% Risk Open $	10% Risk Loss $	10% Risk Close $
1	100,000.00	3,000.00	97,000.00	100,000.00	4,000.00	96,000.00	100,000.00	5,000.00	95,000.00	100,000.00	6,000.00	94,000.00	100,000.00	7,000.00	93,000.00	100,000.00	8,000.00	92,000.00	100,000.00	9,000.00	91,000.00	100,000.00	10,000.00	90,000.00
2	97,000.00	2,910.00	94,090.00	96,000.00	3,840.00	92,160.00	95,000.00	4,750.00	90,250.00	94,000.00	5,640.00	88,360.00	93,000.00	6,510.00	86,490.00	92,000.00	7,360.00	84,640.00	91,000.00	8,190.00	82,810.00	90,000.00	9,000.00	81,000.00
3	94,090.00	2,822.70	91,267.30	92,160.00	3,686.40	88,473.60	90,250.00	4,512.50	85,737.50	88,360.00	5,301.60	83,058.40	86,490.00	6,054.30	80,435.70	84,640.00	6,771.20	77,868.80	82,810.00	7,452.90	75,357.10	81,000.00	8,100.00	72,900.00
4	91,267.30	2,738.02	88,529.28	88,473.60	3,538.94	84,934.66	85,737.50	4,286.88	81,450.63	83,058.40	4,983.50	78,074.90	80,435.70	5,630.50	74,805.20	77,868.80	6,229.50	71,639.30	75,357.10	6,782.14	68,574.96	72,900.00	7,290.00	65,610.00
5	88,529.28	2,655.88	85,873.40	84,934.66	3,397.39	81,537.27	81,450.63	4,072.53	77,378.09	78,074.90	4,684.49	73,390.40	74,805.20	5,236.36	69,568.84	71,639.30	5,731.14	65,908.15	68,574.96	6,171.75	62,403.21	65,610.00	6,561.00	59,049.00
6	85,873.40	2,576.20	83,297.20	81,537.27	3,261.49	78,275.78	77,378.09	3,868.90	73,509.19	73,390.40	4,403.42	68,986.98	69,568.84	4,869.82	64,699.02	65,908.15	5,272.65	60,635.50	62,403.21	5,616.29	56,786.93	59,049.00	5,904.90	53,144.10
7	83,297.20	2,498.92	80,798.28	78,275.78	3,131.03	75,144.75	73,509.19	3,675.46	69,833.73	68,986.98	4,139.22	64,847.76	64,699.02	4,528.93	60,170.09	60,635.50	4,850.84	55,784.66	56,786.93	5,110.82	51,676.10	53,144.10	5,314.41	47,829.69
8	80,798.28	2,423.95	78,374.34	75,144.75	3,005.79	72,138.96	69,833.73	3,491.69	66,342.04	64,847.76	3,890.87	60,956.89	60,170.09	4,211.91	55,958.18	55,784.66	4,462.77	51,321.89	51,676.10	4,650.85	47,025.25	47,829.69	4,782.97	43,046.72
9	78,374.34	2,351.23	76,023.11	72,138.96	2,885.56	69,253.40	66,342.04	3,317.10	63,024.94	60,956.89	3,657.41	57,299.48	55,958.18	3,917.07	52,041.11	51,321.89	4,105.75	47,216.14	47,025.25	4,232.27	42,792.98	43,046.72	4,304.67	38,742.05
10	76,023.11	2,280.69	73,742.41	69,253.40	2,770.14	66,483.26	63,024.94	3,151.25	59,873.69	57,299.48	3,437.97	53,861.51	52,041.11	3,642.88	48,398.23	47,216.14	3,777.29	43,438.85	42,792.98	3,851.37	38,941.61	38,742.05	3,874.20	34,867.84
11	73,742.41	2,212.27	71,530.14	66,483.26	2,659.33	63,823.93	59,873.69	2,993.68	56,880.01	53,861.51	3,231.69	50,629.82	48,398.23	3,387.88	45,010.35	43,438.85	3,475.11	39,963.74	38,941.61	3,504.75	35,436.87	34,867.84	3,486.78	31,381.06
12	71,530.14	2,145.90	69,384.24	63,823.93	2,552.96	61,270.98	56,880.01	2,844.00	54,036.01	50,629.82	3,037.79	47,592.03	45,010.35	3,150.72	41,859.63	39,963.74	3,197.10	36,766.64	35,436.87	3,189.32	32,247.55	31,381.06	3,138.11	28,242.95
13	69,384.24	2,081.53	67,302.71	61,270.98	2,450.84	58,820.14	54,036.01	2,701.80	51,334.21	47,592.03	2,855.52	44,736.51	41,859.63	2,930.17	38,929.46	36,766.64	2,941.33	33,825.31	32,247.55	2,902.28	29,345.27	28,242.95	2,824.30	25,418.66
14	67,302.71	2,019.08	65,283.63	58,820.14	2,352.81	56,467.33	51,334.21	2,566.71	48,767.50	44,736.51	2,684.19	42,052.32	38,929.46	2,725.06	36,204.39	33,825.31	2,706.02	31,119.28	29,345.27	2,641.07	26,704.20	25,418.66	2,541.87	22,876.79
15	65,283.63	1,958.51	63,325.12	56,467.33	2,258.69	54,208.64	48,767.50	2,438.37	46,329.12	42,052.32	2,523.14	39,529.18	36,204.39	2,534.31	33,670.09	31,119.28	2,489.54	28,629.74	26,704.20	2,403.38	24,300.82	22,876.79	2,287.68	20,589.11
16	63,325.12	1,899.75	61,425.37	54,208.64	2,168.35	52,040.29	46,329.12	2,316.46	44,012.67	39,529.18	2,371.75	37,157.43	33,670.09	2,356.91	31,313.18	28,629.74	2,290.38	26,339.36	24,300.82	2,187.07	22,113.74	20,589.11	2,058.91	18,530.20
17	61,425.37	1,842.76	59,582.60	52,040.29	2,081.61	49,958.68	44,012.67	2,200.63	41,812.03	37,157.43	2,229.45	34,927.98	31,313.18	2,191.92	29,121.26	26,339.36	2,107.15	24,232.21	22,113.74	1,990.24	20,123.51	18,530.20	1,853.02	16,677.18
18	59,582.60	1,787.48	57,795.13	49,958.68	1,998.35	47,960.33	41,812.03	2,090.60	39,721.43	34,927.98	2,095.68	32,832.30	29,121.26	2,038.49	27,082.77	24,232.21	1,938.58	22,293.64	20,123.51	1,811.12	18,312.39	16,677.18	1,667.72	15,009.46
19	57,795.13	1,733.85	56,061.27	47,960.33	1,918.41	46,041.92	39,721.43	1,986.07	37,735.36	32,832.30	1,969.94	30,862.37	27,082.77	1,895.79	25,186.98	22,293.64	1,783.49	20,510.14	18,312.39	1,648.12	16,664.28	15,009.46	1,500.95	13,508.52
20	56,061.27	1,681.84	54,379.43	46,041.92	1,841.68	44,200.24	37,735.36	1,886.77	35,848.59	30,862.37	1,851.74	29,010.62	25,186.98	1,763.09	23,423.89	20,510.14	1,640.81	18,869.33	16,664.28	1,499.78	15,164.49	13,508.52	1,350.85	12,157.67
21	54,379.43	1,631.38	52,748.05	44,200.24	1,768.01	42,432.23	35,848.59	1,792.43	34,056.16	29,010.62	1,740.64	27,269.99	23,423.89	1,639.67	21,784.22	18,869.33	1,509.55	17,359.79	15,164.49	1,364.80	13,799.69	12,157.67	1,215.77	10,941.90
22	52,748.05	1,582.44	51,165.61	42,432.23	1,697.29	40,734.94	34,056.16	1,702.81	32,353.35	27,269.99	1,636.20	25,633.79	21,784.22	1,524.90	20,259.32	17,359.79	1,388.78	15,971.00	13,799.69	1,241.97	12,557.72	10,941.90	1,094.19	9,847.71
23	51,165.61	1,534.97	49,630.64	40,734.94	1,629.40	39,105.55	32,353.35	1,617.67	30,735.69	25,633.79	1,538.03	24,095.76	20,259.32	1,418.15	18,841.17	15,971.00	1,277.68	14,693.32	12,557.72	1,130.19	11,427.52	9,847.71	984.77	8,862.94
24	49,630.64	1,488.92	48,141.72	39,105.55	1,564.22	37,541.32	30,735.69	1,536.78	29,198.90	24,095.76	1,445.75	22,650.01	18,841.17	1,318.88	17,522.29	14,693.32	1,175.47	13,517.86	11,427.52	1,028.48	10,399.04	8,862.94	886.29	7,976.64
25	48,141.72	1,444.25	46,697.47	37,541.32	1,501.65	36,039.67	29,198.90	1,459.95	27,738.96	22,650.01	1,359.00	21,291.01	17,522.29	1,226.56	16,295.73	13,517.86	1,081.43	12,436.43	10,399.04	935.91	9,463.13	7,976.64	797.66	7,178.98
26	46,697.47	1,400.92	45,296.55	36,039.67	1,441.59	34,598.08	27,738.96	1,386.95	26,352.01	21,291.01	1,277.46	20,013.55	16,295.73	1,140.70	15,155.03	12,436.43	994.91	11,441.51	9,463.13	851.68	8,611.45	7,178.98	717.90	6,461.08
27	45,296.55	1,358.90	43,937.65	34,598.08	1,383.92	33,214.16	26,352.01	1,317.60	25,034.41	20,013.55	1,200.81	18,812.74	15,155.03	1,060.85	14,094.17	11,441.51	915.32	10,526.19	8,611.45	775.03	7,836.42	6,461.08	646.11	5,814.97
28	43,937.65	1,318.13	42,619.52	33,214.16	1,328.57	31,885.59	25,034.41	1,251.72	23,782.69	18,812.74	1,128.76	17,683.98	14,094.17	986.59	13,107.58	10,526.19	842.10	9,684.10	7,836.42	705.28	7,131.14	5,814.97	581.50	5,233.48
29	42,619.52	1,278.59	41,340.93	31,885.59	1,275.42	30,610.17	23,782.69	1,189.13	22,593.55	17,683.98	1,061.04	16,622.94	13,107.58	917.53	12,190.05	9,684.10	774.73	8,909.37	7,131.14	641.80	6,489.34	5,233.48	523.35	4,710.13
30	41,340.93	1,240.23	40,100.71	30,610.17	1,224.41	29,385.76	22,593.55	1,129.68	21,463.88	16,622.94	997.38	15,625.56	12,190.05	853.30	11,336.75	8,909.37	712.75	8,196.62	6,489.34	584.04	5,905.30	4,710.13	471.01	4,239.12
31	40,100.71	1,203.02	38,897.69	29,385.76	1,175.43	28,210.33	21,463.88	1,073.19	20,390.68	15,625.56	937.53	14,688.03	11,336.75	793.57	10,543.17	8,196.62	655.73	7,540.89	5,905.30	531.48	5,373.82	4,239.12	423.91	3,815.20

FIGURE 8: SPREADSHEET SHOWING THE ACCUMULATED LOSS WHEN THE PERCENTAGE RISK IS INCREASED ON A $100K ACCOUNT

Regardless of the account size we are trading, it would take 69 consecutive losses for a 1% risk to wipe out half our account, whereas a 5% risk would achieve that in just 14 losing trades.

Dr. Alexander Elder trained as a medical doctor in the former Soviet Union and later worked as a psychiatrist in New York. He also taught at Columbia University, before going on to become a professional trader. Dr. Elder is the author of numerous books on trading including the bestseller, *The New Trading for a Living*.[5] He tells us: "Extensive testing has shown that the maximum amount a trader may lose on a single trade without damaging his long-term prospects is 2 percent of his equity."

This means a trader with a $20,000 account, risking the maximum of 2%, must expose no more than $400 per trade. Traders with large accounts risk less, and 0.5% is not uncommon. Beginners should risk a maximum of 1% per trade, and when comfortable with that they shouldn't go immediately to 2% (a 100% increase in risk): 1.25% should be next.

Beginners are always surprised to discover that most of the profits made during a year's trading can come from just a few good trades. The rest of the time we concentrate on preserving our capital by taking a series of small losses. If a boxer can defend himself well, he has to suffer a few small jabs, but he will eventually get the chance to land a big punch.

When we lose money our instinct is to risk more in the next trade in the hope of reversing recent losses with larger gains. In fact, we must do the opposite and reduce our capital at risk. This process of constantly reducing our risk operates in the same way as amortized

---

5   Elder, Dr. Alexander, *The New Trading for a Living: Psychology, Discipline, Trading Tools and Systems, Risk Control, Trade Management*, Wiley Trading, ISBN 978-1118443927.

loan repayments. The numerical size of each losing payment to the market reduces as the balance of our account decreases.

It's also helpful to see the risk in terms of a round number rather than a set percentage. Percentages are fine in theory, but we relate better to round numbers. We need to be able to say, "*Well, if that trade doesn't work out, I have only lost $400,*" with 'only' being the operative word.

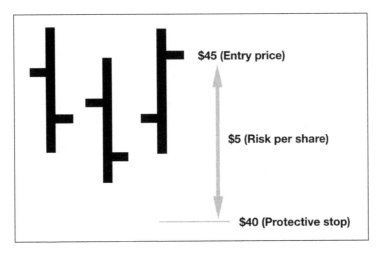

FIGURE 9: RISK CALCULATION USING ENTRY PRICE AND PROTECTIVE STOP WHEN ENTERING A TRADE

To calculate our exposure on each trade we only need two figures: our entry price and our exit price. The difference between them in cash terms is our risk. For example, if we plan to enter a trade at $45 and get out if it falls to $40, our exposure is $5 per share. If we are risking $1,000 per trade, then we divide that by our risk per share and we can buy 200 shares or less. The 200 shares will cost $9,000. If the trade doesn't work out and we exit at $40, we will get back $8,000 (less a few dollars commission) and suffer our maximum loss of $1,000.

Notice we decide the entry and exit prices first and then decide the number of shares to trade, not the other way around. Our entry and exit should be the same regardless of the account size we are trading. In the example used, a risk of $1,000 allows us to buy 200 shares. Someone taking the exact same trade while trading a $10m account, and risking 0.5% per trade ($50,000), would also enter at $45 and exit at $40, but they would buy 10,000 shares.

In the **Ten Tools** chapter we will be taking a closer look at orders which allow us to manage our risk effectively – the most important of which is a protective stop.

(c) THE 6% LIMIT

Kerrich's coin experiment showed how a string of identical results can randomly occur and the 6% limit breaks the string if we are caught in a series of loss-making trades.

In *Come Into My Trading Room*,[6] Dr. Elder suggests we should set a monthly limit of 6% for our losses and stop trading for the remainder of the month if we hit that amount. Depending on our trading style, this can be a calendar month or a rolling 30-day period. This break will call a halt to a losing streak and give us time to cool off and reassess the market. It also means a trader risking 2% per trade will be on the bench after three consecutive strikes.

In **The Strategies** chapter we will look at 12 years trading results for the Help-Up Strategy and see how the 6% rule kicked in on four occasions.

(d) THE 20% LIMIT

Next we need to consider the possibility of a one-off major loss. If we get a very good entry on a trade or we are trading a stock with a high price, we can unknowingly take on an oversized position while still observing the 2% and 6% limits.

For example, if we buy a stock at $810 and have a protective stop at $790, we are risking $20 per share. Assuming 2% risk on a $100,000

---

6   Elder Dr. Alexander, *Come Into My Trading Room: A Complete Guide to Trading*, Wiley, ISBN 978-0-471-225348.

account, we could buy 100 shares. This will cost us $81,000 (81% of our entire account balance), but we are still risking just 2% of our account.

What happens if the stock gaps down at the open on an unexpected event and starts trading at $695? We have lost over 11% of our account because we had too much money in one single position. For this reason, we also limit our exposure on any single trade to a maximum of 20% of our entire account to avoid so-called **concentration risk**.

Therefore, in the example above we should buy no more than 24 shares (20% of our account balance divided by the share price and rounded down). Following the sudden drop in price, our 24 shares would give us a total loss of $2,760, which is just 2.76% of our account, even though the share price dropped over 14%.

(e) THE 40% LIMIT

A core element of any profitable trading strategy is the **risk/reward ratio** (RRR). In simple terms, the potential risk in a trade needs to be significantly less than the potential reward, and the ratio should be no greater than 1/2.5 or 40%. By applying this rule, using a constant risk size, we can lose more than half the time but still be a net winner in the long run, because a handful of large gains more than compensates for all the small losses.

It's important to understand the RRR on a trade can only be calculated after the trade is closed – because we never know in advance how profitable a trade will be. Whenever I hear traders talking about 'price targets', it reminds me of when we were kids and told each other we would be millionaires when we grew up. Sticking unrealistic targets on a trade in order to convince ourselves we have the necessary RRR is a common rookie mistake. Moving up a protective stop to rebalance the ratio is the other.

For trend followers, predicting a RRR in advance of a trade is meaningless because a good trend always lasts longer than anticipated.

The reward side of the ratio is not set in stone and if the target is not reached or exceeded, it's OK. The limit exists to make us think about a trade before entering rather than creating a defined target at which we must get out, or a level that has to be reached before taking profits.

Summary of the five limits of risk

We have now established how to assess the risk in a trade and how to manage it using the following five limits of risk:

(a) 1% (maximum position size relative to a stock's daily turnover)

(b) 2% (maximum risk in any individual trade)

(c) 6% (maximum monthly drawdown on our account)

(d) 20% (maximum exposure in any single position)

(e) 40% (maximum risk-to-reward ratio).

Ongoing risk management

We should avoid the temptation to micromanage the balance in our account by watching the figure tick up and down throughout the day. Forget about the money. We know our losses are controlled, so we have nothing to worry about and we can focus on the task at hand. Once we have a defined structure to our risk-assessment process, we are not afraid to embrace risk with confidence because we know our account can handle the fallout.

As we have seen, calculating our risk when opening trades is not a problem. The difficulty arises when we have been in a profitable trade for a while and we start opening more trades or alter the size of our current positions. In these circumstances, monitoring our risk on an ongoing basis can be a challenge.

Soon we will look at the **Eight Checks** we perform each day before trading and these include a risk management section which addresses the issue.

Risk-induced anxiety

The management of risk is not just about numbers. We must also bear risk on a mental and emotional level. There is little point in risking 2% of our account on trades if we can't sleep at night. The risk tolerance for individual traders is different and we need to figure out how much we can risk and still function normally.

If we are uneasy about a position, we should reduce the size of the trade by selling some shares until we are down to a level where we are not constantly thinking about it, even if this means we only have $100 invested. When we are comfortable operating at that level, we should slowly increase the funds at risk as our confidence and experience grows.

3. Responsibility

Ideally, every trader should serve an apprenticeship of four to five years. In the real world, it doesn't happen like that. Private traders (including this author) take the highly irresponsible approach of trying to educate themselves and end up paying the price.

There is an accepted understanding that we all have basic human rights, but our basic human responsibilities are conveniently overlooked, especially the responsibility we have to ourselves and our family to make the best use of the financial resources at our disposal.

Traders must step up to the plate and take full responsibility for everything they do in the market and this happens in three ways:

(a) A trading coach

When a trader blames everything but themselves for their losses, while taking full responsibility for their gains, they learn nothing. As a result, they get trapped in a self-perpetuating cycle of frustrated misunderstanding which ultimately destroys their account. They cannot solve this problem alone – someone outside the destructive cycle has to show them the solution.

One of the best ways to take responsibility for our trading is to make ourselves responsible to others. For example, if we need to have a certain setup in place before we enter a trade, we are more likely to follow our strategies if we know we'll have to explain our actions to someone later on, and this is where a trading coach or mentor comes in.

In the markets, there is an ingenious pricing model for education. The fee is directly proportional to our resistance to learn. The more stubborn we are, the more it will cost. As the 2010 study of the Taiwan Stock Exchange confirmed, 'trading to learn' simply doesn't work.

In addition, the French report stated in the conclusion, "… investors who trade the most… lose the most. The same applies to those who continue over time, indicating there is no learning curve."

A clever person learns from their mistakes, a wise one learns from the mistakes of others. Why struggle to reinvent the market wheel, when we can discover everything we need from others who have already been through the process?

If we are serious about trading, we need to get some good training. We need exposure to experienced traders and come to understand what they do and how they do it. This will require a certain amount of trust, some money, and a lot of time.

Beginners often have a resistance to paying a trading coach. In my case, I thought of the old tradesman's saying, 'Those who can, do, and those who can't, teach.' It occurred to me, if these guys are so good at trading, why are they giving classes (and writing books) when they could be making a fortune in the market?

This is a popular question among beginners (or the more suspicious ones anyway) and demonstrates a basic lack of understanding of the trading profession. Some of the most successful traders don't spend a lot of time every day in front of the screen. Yet they need to stay in touch with the market and keep their skills sharp. Teaching others to trade is one of the best ways to do this, because it forces the teacher to have a thorough knowledge of the subject and to practice what they preach.

Individual traders have very different life experiences and personalities, so they will sometimes have an approach to the markets not previously considered by the teacher. In addition, new social trends and perspectives tend to evolve from the ground up, so interaction with a wide range of students benefits the teacher as much as the class.

There is also an important social aspect to this relationship, as informal groups often crystallize among practitioners of a particular trading style. Good instructors realize there is no monopoly on trading skill, and the best trader they will ever meet might be sitting in front of them tomorrow.

Fantastic traders often lack the ability to transfer their knowledge to others, just as stars of the sports field can struggle with the transition to coaching. On the other hand, some of the best sports coaches in the world were just average performers in their day. The skill set required for coaching is different from the requirements on the field. We might have the potential to be a great trader, but it could take an average trader who is a great coach to unlock it for us.

One final comment on the subject, and something to watch out for when looking for coaches and mentors: someone who makes confident and convincing predictions about the market will be just as confident and convincing as they explain why it didn't happen. If they make enough predictions, some will be right. After all, even a stopped clock is correct twice a day.

Traders need coaches who work with probabilities and accept the limitations of the process. The job of a coach is to train others how to do the same and allow traders to take full responsibility for their actions. It's not a coach's job to supply us with trade ideas.

(b) Trading records

As we saw earlier, good records are what separate successful traders from gamblers. Records are the practical application of trading responsibility and they must be honest and factual if they are going to serve their purpose. Since good records are an essential component of trading, we will look at them separately in the **Seven Records** chapter.

(c) Market karma

The final part of responsible trading relates to the non-financial impact of our orders. In everyday life, we wouldn't go around mindlessly making decisions which affect others without considering the consequences. If we did, we would soon find ourselves in hot water.

Every single thing we do in life has an impact on someone or something. For the most part, it's harmless, but sometimes the smallest thing matters. As the saying goes, 'Even a tiny spark can burn down a mountain of hay.'

A book on trading is the last place one would expect to find a lecture on morality, so you won't find it here. However, for those who think about such things, in the **Nine Filters** chapter we will see how to screen for stocks which may be in conflict with our moral beliefs.

4. Routine

The experience of new traders could be summed up as: confusion and frustration. They have to make decisions in an uncertain environment, while also being unsure of themselves. It feels like being a teenager all over again, but without the parents to clean up the mess.

The key to making profitable decisions in the market is a trading strategy. The advantage of a strategy is improved profitability, but equally important is the fact that we always know what to do. By following a strategy, we remove the potential of a strong emotional response to the outcome of any trade, as we see the results in terms of 'the strategy' rather than 'my decisions.'

When I began to work with professional traders, I was surprised to discover they were trading the exact same stocks as me, but they were making a profit because they were following a routine which allowed them to manage their trades better. All profitable trading routines have a handful of strategies at their heart.

Trading strategies

Having identified our preferred style, we need to learn specific strategies to trade within that style. A good strategy must have a proven track record supported by comprehensive backtested results. Developing our own strategies and backtesting them is a time-consuming process.

With the possible exception of automated and algorithmic trading, there have been very few developments within trading strategies in recent times. Even the Fibonacci number sequence (used by traders to locate reversal points and price targets) was used in Indian society around 400BC.[7] Candlestick charts, another favorite among the techies, are believed to have been used in Japan in the late 1800s.[8] These tools have proven their worth by their longevity. Trading strategies are the same. We just need to choose one and use it consistently.

A good strategy allows us to face the market with confidence and composure. Confidence is vital among traders, but it's not so much about

---

7   Singh, Parmanand, 'The So-called Fibonacci numbers in ancient and medieval India', *Historia Mathematica*, 1985, 12 (3): 229–44, (doi:10.1016/0315-0860(85)90021-7).

8   Nison, Steve, *Beyond Candlesticks: New Japanese Charting Techniques Revealed*, ISBN 978-0-471-00720-3.

having confidence in the strategy, it's more about having confidence in ourselves to follow it. Most strategies are pretty straightforward – the weakness lies in the person trading them.

If we are in the habit of placing impulsive trades, we will keep getting into situations we should never be in. Likewise, if we are in a good trade, impulsive behavior will cause us to close it out when it goes on to be highly profitable. The solution to all of this is a documented strategy which only allows us to enter and exit trades when we can check all the boxes.

We should be able to write down each strategy we trade so that another trader can clearly understand it without further clarification. If we can't do that, then we are not trading a proper strategy. At a bare minimum, our strategy should clearly identify how and when we enter a trade, how we manage it once we are in and what needs to happen (or not happen) for us to exit. At no stage during the process should we be confused about what to do.

If our favorite strategy is not working out as we expect, do we fine-tune it? This throws up another challenge, because strategies are so easy to play around with. The settings on our technical indicators are simple to alter, which means we are tempted to form the tool while still using it.

Robert Prechter summed up this problem nicely when he wrote, "Most traders take a good system and destroy it by trying to make it into a perfect system." If our trading is profitable, our system is already perfect, and we should leave it alone and work on ourselves.

Some profitable strategies have a success rate as low as 40%. This means the majority of our trades will be 'losers' and the profitable trades can be erratic and unexpected. The 'winning' trades, when they occur, can often feel like a fluke. But when flukes keep happening, the strategy is profitable. The only way we realize this is to stay consistent with our routine.

Strategies look great in a small book, but they often crumble when they make it to the big screen. In addition, different traders using the same strategy in the same market can often have wildly different results. It's a case of matching the strategy to the personality. To fully master a trading strategy, we have to be brought through the process step by step and then trade it ourselves under close adult supervision.

Trading signals

Every good strategy should have a number of clearly defined requirements which must be met before we can proceed with a trade. This will normally be technical indicators giving the signals we require. We should think of these signals as the dials on a combination lock. When all the numbers are correct, and the wheels aligned, only then is the market door open to us.

We will be looking at signals in more detail in the **Ten Tools** chapter and again in **Part C**, but it's important to be aware each strategy should have a primary signal around which the strategy is based. If it's a trend-following strategy, a lagging indicator such as a moving average is useful. For swing trading, oscillators which fluctuate above and below a centre line are best. In addition to the primary signal there should be at least one supporting signal and possibly more (but not too many). The supporting signals should be indicators capturing a different market perspective, rather than repeating the message of the primary one.

Conclusion

Beginners spend far too much time on the **routine** of strategies and technical indicators, when they should be concentrating on the application of **reason** and the control of **risk**. The money is made and lost on these two, but they get the least attention. As for number three – **responsibility** for ourselves and our decisions – this tends to be totally ignored.

FIVE STAGES

*The Path of a Successful
Trader's Career*

T HERE IS A clear and well-trodden road which successful
traders follow. When we break the journey down into its
five stages, it's not as daunting as it first appears.

1. Reckless

In the 80s, I frequented a nightclub which used the catchphrase, '*Where
love stories begin.*' When the receivers entered the building a few years
later, they had a different story in mind. The love affair of a new trader
with the market inevitably begins with romantic recklessness. It certainly
did in my case, and the rose of romance had some sharp thorns.

When I started to trade, I was constantly jumping from one market
to another, trading different instruments in my quest to make a quick
fortune. I switched from one style to the next and tried four different
trading platforms. I was always on edge and constantly checking my
open positions. The manic hosts on financial news channels played more
havoc with my emotions than any young thing in legwarmers ever did.

Looking back on those days, the only thing that kept me out of trouble was my preference for equities and an instinct for frugality. Thankfully, I wasn't one for 'Hail Mary' trades, where a trader goes all in on a hunch and a prayer. This type of trading leads to disastrous losses which wipe out many beginners.

Losing money

It's important we lose money when we start trading. In fact, it's an essential job requirement. Losses are the entrance fee to the profession and the more we lose the better the interview went. Dealing with loss is the apprenticeship of trading, the tough grind we all have to endure when we start a new career.

Our acceptance and understanding of loss is the bedrock on which our future success will be built. Regrettably many traders fail to understand the significance of this early learning opportunity.

When a beginner makes money, it can have worse consequences. If he makes a month's wages in a few trades, he begins to lose interest in his day job and considers taking up trading full time. The warm feeling he experiences as he counts his winnings is not the glow of success, it's the breeze of the bullet which just passed his head. Flush with cash, he starts increasing his position size and risk. All the while, turning his account into a bigger target, ensuring the professionals won't miss next time.

2. Recognition

When I met other traders, the story was the same all over. The honest beginners were losing money, the rest were either too embarrassed to admit it or too lazy to change. It was fascinating to see the diversity of cultural and educational backgrounds, yet in spite of our different approaches to the market we all ended up in the same hole.

The first thing a paramedic does when he arrives at the scene of an accident is to stop the bleeding. Likewise, once we recognize we have been trading recklessly, we need to stop the cash bleeding from our account. To do this we need to stop trading.

Excessive trading is one of the leading causes of mortality among newly opened trading accounts. What's worse, traders don't 'lose' money – it is taken from them. Their losses don't flow down a drain in Wall Street, they flow into the accounts of other traders. Every day billions of dollars change hands, flowing from thousands of accounts held by amateurs into hundreds of accounts held by professionals. When losers stop trading, winners stop taking.

A bad trader is like a bad negotiator, every time he sits down at the table he gets a worse deal.

For beginners, this is where things start to get difficult because they need to accept they are out of their depth. This can be a bitter pill to swallow for mature and intelligent people.

The Dunning-Kruger effect[1]

In 1999, two American social psychologists, Justin Kruger and David Dunning, conducted a series of tests on 65 undergraduate students at Cornell University. The students were tested on humor, logical reasoning and English grammar, and were then asked to assess their own ability in the tests. The study concluded that when people think they are good at something, but are not, they fail to recognize their own ineptitude.

In their final report, Dunning and Kruger state:

---

1   *Unskilled and Unaware of It: How Difficulties in Recognizing One's Own Incompetence Lead to Inflated Self-Assessments* (citeseerx.ist.psu.edu/viewdoc/download?doi=10.1.1.64.2655&rep=rep1&type=pdf).

"We propose that those with limited knowledge in a domain suffer a dual burden: Not only do they reach mistaken conclusions and make regrettable errors, but their incompetence robs them of the ability to realize it."

If ever there was a definition of reckless trading, that is it.

3. Revival

Once a losing trader has stopped trading, they need to take some time out and make a decision. They can embark on the road to **revival**, which will involve effort and patience, or they can give up trading altogether. These are the only **two choices** which will preserve the capital left in their account.

Should they choose revival, they need to do the following:

(a) Realistically assess their ability to trade.

(b) Accept a reasonable return on investment.

(c) Identify the market they will trade.

(d) Find a trading style which suits their personality, lifestyle and resources.

(e) Learn a trading strategy with a proven profitable outcome.

(f) Constantly apply risk management tools.

(g) Keep good records.

(h) Stay humble and keep an open mind.

As they start trading again with their new rules and records, their account balance will stop falling, but it probably won't start rising either – at least not straightaway. This is common and is actually a very good sign. It is the first indication they are making progress. They are trading but not losing as much as before – their risk management tools are working.

Things get a little more challenging as the revival continues, because the transition to profitability requires experience and skill. It's not just a case of flapping their trading wings, they have to learn how to fly. Listed below, in no particular order, are some of the flying lessons I attended:

(a) Elbow grease

When we cook a roast or wash our clothes, we don't actually 'cook' or 'wash' anything. We arrange the infrastructure and create the circumstances which allow it to happen. The properties of the heat do the cooking and the composition of the water does the washing, we just facilitate the event.

In the same way, we don't 'make' money from trading. We arrange a financial infrastructure and create circumstances which allow our account to benefit from inherent opportunities in the market. Making money is a side effect of our activity – not the activity itself.

Building an infrastructure which will essentially pull money out of thin air when the circumstances are right, requires a lot of time and effort on our part. This will involve backtesting strategies, keeping records, attending courses and events, finding and manually entering data, reading reports and generally educating ourselves on the markets. These humdrum activities are not very glamorous, but they are the pots and pans of trading.

After a long day on the road or in the office, the idea of facing our trading job after work may not sound very appealing. This is especially the case if we have a few pastimes on the go or we have a partner and kids who require our time. Trying to fit our trading into a busy schedule can be very stressful, so we may be inclined to take shortcuts.

It's very tempting to throw a few trades into the market when we are busy, just to be active or to stay in touch, but this is gambling. Each trade we place in the market should be the end result of a process, not the beginning. If we are not prepared (or not able) to do the necessary homework before we trade, we are better off not trading until our circumstances change.

(b) Equipment

Despite the ubiquitous image of traders sitting in front of a bank of screens, we only need one. A large screen (24–27") is sufficient to view everything simultaneously with all the level of detail required. If we are working from a laptop, we can use an external monitor.

A good laptop is an essential tool for private traders. One of the 'ultrabook' models with a screen size of at least 15", high resolution and the fastest processor we can afford, is what's required. Personally, I use a MacBook Pro and run Windows on it with a virtual machine.

(c) Predictions

A common error among beginners is falling into the habit of market predictions. When this type of thinking informs our trading decisions, we are setting ourselves up for some serious losses. We must constantly remind ourselves to stop anticipating what is going to happen, because anything (or nothing) (or everything) could happen next.

We know the market moves in recurring patterns. Rather than wasting our time predicting the future direction of the market, we should spend the time more productively by learning how to recognize those patterns and have a plan to trade them when they occur.

Embarrassment is a wonderful motivator and we should use it to our advantage. If we are in the habit of making predictions, we should make them loud and clear and tell everyone (maybe we should even start a blog). That way when our predictions don't come true, hopefully the embarrassment will be so overwhelming that we stop making predictions.

(d) Expertise

Some people believe 10,000 hours spent on a topic makes them an expert. That's not the case in the market. Sooner or later, 'trading experts' become complacent and predictable, and that's when the market snaps them back to reality.

The renowned Japanese teacher Shunryu Suzuki-Roshi, tells us: "In the beginner's mind there are many possibilities. In the expert's mind, there are few."[2] Anything is possible in the market and every day is essentially the first day – therefore a true market expert always sees themselves as a beginner.

(e) Smart money

Some traders believe the market is rigged against them and this opinion usually arises after a series of losses. A Machiavellian conspiracy of that magnitude would require organization, but the global financial system is more chaotic than it appears. Large financial firms are often so consumed with internal issues, they have neither the time nor the focus to maintain a conspiracy. If we believe we are being impeded by rigging, we should look at the masts on our own ship first.

Just as the sea doesn't differentiate between a giant ocean-going trawler and a small coastal fishing boat, the rising and falling market tide treats everyone with equal indifference, so we have as good a chance as anyone else – large or small.

If we are not beating the market, we shouldn't get too despondent – we are in good company. Every six months, S&P Dow Jones Indices produce the SPIVA Scorecard,[3] which "compares actively managed funds against their appropriate benchmarks on a semiannual basis."

---

2   Shunryu, Suzuki, *Zen Mind, Beginner's Mind*, Shambhala Publications Inc., 2011, ISBN-13: 978-1590308493.

3   S&P Dow Jones Indices, SPIVA® Reports, data as of 29 December 2017 (us.spindices.com/spiva/#/reports).

According to data as of 29 December 2017, 84.23% of large-cap funds in the U.S. underperformed the S&P 500 index for the previous five years. European funds fared a little better, where only 73.26% were outperformed by the S&P Europe 350. In Australia, 68.69% underperformed their benchmark index. Japan and India were the best performers where 44.31% and 43.4% failed to match their home indices.

There is much talk in the markets about 'smart money' and 'dumb money'. Supposedly big money managers are smart and retail guys are on the slow side. To my mind, the only thing smart about institutions is the fact that they are usually using someone else's money. When one has to rely exclusively on trading performance to pay the bills (as private traders do), managing the funds of others, for a fee, seems like the smart thing to do.

(f) Et tu, Brute?

There are certain times in history when enormous change takes place very quickly. These short and intense moments of disruption and chaos define everything for years to come. While these events can prove challenging for those involved, they also provide unique opportunities if we have the wisdom to recognize them and the courage to exploit them.

War is a perfect example. Social structures and national borders which have existed for generations are instantly wiped out and created anew. Politicians and generals know more can be achieved in a few days on the battlefield than decades spent in negotiations at the UN. In battle, there are no rules and no boundaries: the process creates new ones. So, they grab the opportunity with both hands and exploit it to the maximum.

The markets are a constant battle of financial disruption and chaos. In the struggle between market participants, everything changes in an instant and it has lasting financial consequences for everyone. This is a very challenging environment in which to operate, but this is also the place where golden opportunities are born if we can act in a manner which is structured.

Shakespeare put it more poetically in *Julius Caesar* when Brutus says:

> "There is a tide in the affairs of men,
> Which taken at the flood,
> leads on to fortune.
> Omitted, all the voyage of their life,
> Is bound in shallows and in miseries.
> On such a full sea are we now afloat,
> And we must take the current when it serves,
> Or lose our ventures."[4]

These eight lines perfectly encapsulate the inherent opportunity of the market. This flooding tide of finance is not an easy place to be, but it leads on to fortune if we know how to navigate it. Traders must have the courage to grab their charts and set sail on the market tide.

(g) The market engine

Money is never allowed to rest in peace and its owners are constantly engaged in a 'search for yield'. For amateur investors and traders, this usually involves going from a position in cash to a listed instrument and back again. However, these are just two of the six main asset classes we should be familiar with, as follows:

1. equities (publicly listed stocks and shares)

2. fixed income (bonds and other debt)

3. cash (hard currencies)

4. real estate (actual property or a fund)

5. commodities (physical or ETFs)

---

4   Shakespeare, William, *Julius Caesar*, Palala Press, 2016, ISBN-13: 978-1355470489.

6. alternatives (anything which isn't the other five, e.g. art, wine, private equity, forestry).

The classic example used to describe the movement of assets is a six-cylinder internal combustion engine, where assets are the pistons constantly rising and falling relative to each other. Rather than jumping off the cylinder block (cash) onto the same piston each time (equities) and back again, we should consider jumping from piston to piston.

Experienced investors ride each asset to the top of its cycle and jump over to another one when they see it is starting to rise. They understand the shape of the market crankshaft – the mood which is driving the global financial engine – so they know which will be rising next.

(h) Suspended in space

Every year, a group of friends and I charter a boat in the Red Sea which sleeps 16 scuba divers and crew along with all our gear. We cruise up and down the Egyptian coast, exploring shipwrecks and watching sharks and turtles on the beautiful coral reefs. These calm and azure waters come as a pleasant surprise to British and Irish divers who are used to underwater rock climbing in the murky and stormy seas of the North Atlantic.

We begin the week by descending and ascending on a rope which is anchored to the seabed. As the week progresses, we have to do 'free ascents' in open water, which means we come to the surface with no reference points. This can be very challenging for the new divers among us, because they trained in conditions where rocky outcrops and swaying kelp were always present. But now they are suspended in space with nothing solid to guide them.

Floating weightless in this three-dimensional crystal-clear space challenges all our senses. Everything fixed is gone, while the sound of our breathing is magnified, so we can easily become disoriented. This spatial disorientation also happens to pilots when flying through clouds. The solution is to be trained on instruments and give priority to that information rather than our senses.

The confusing mental experience is very similar to the environment we encounter in the market because everything solid is gone. But market disorientation is worse than diving or flying, because we make the error of thinking historical price action on our charts is solid rocky ground. We think we can hold onto it and it's going to continue as before.

Experienced traders have learned to operate comfortably in this strange world. They know every line on a chart could potentially have been a different line, they see no contradiction between the fixed and the fluid. Like a jellyfish suspended in saline space, they're content to go where the tide takes them; not seeking something solid, they can't become disorientated.

The market is constantly forming and dissolving anew. It opens in the unknown and closes without answers. We will never truly understand the market and we should stop trying. This just magnifies the disorientation. Instead, we should concentrate on the message of our technical indicators and give less credence to other stimuli.

This will help greatly, but we also need to accept the limitations of our indicators and back them up with common sense and risk management. Our diving computer won't tell us we're in shark-infested waters and our flight instruments don't know the airline declared bankruptcy. Likewise, our technical indicators don't know when a share price is being manipulated or the accountants have been attending creative writing classes.

(i) Perpetual emotional motion

Increasingly, events are defined not by their actual impact on our lives, but on how we feel about them. It's as if things are not 'real' unless we have an emotional response, and the stronger the emotion the better.

Perhaps this is a reaction to a more organized world, where we feel we have been reduced to a number on a database. Numbers don't laugh, cry or get angry, therefore if we respond emotionally we feel we have confirmed our humanity.

Part of the blame must go to 'reality' TV shows. This artificial construct examines the human condition from the perspective of an emotional voyeur, and the reality is not real until someone breaks down crying – again. All of this validates the supposed power of emotion and reinforces the narrative that a strong emotional response to a difficult situation is the ultimate escape, *"Turn off the camera, I am too upset to talk right now!"*

Like a long-running soap opera, the markets are caught in perpetual emotional motion and the best traders observe the never-ending drama from the detached vantage point of a seasoned cameraman. It's not that they have the mindset of a sociopath or an automaton – they just place the activity of trading in its correct emotional context.

When logic and reason fail us and we default to an emotional defense, trading becomes very difficult. If emotion is our starting point, all hope of profitability is lost. We are supposed to invest and trade our money in the market, but we end up investing our emotions as well. In so doing, we allow the market to hold us hostage and we keep having to pay a ransom.

If we are unfortunate enough to be burdened with above-average emotions, we need to grow less attached to them. The market is a great place to put our money, but it always offers a negative return on emotional investments.

We should be able to consistently trade our strategies when we are happy or sad, elated or depressed. Our mental and emotional experience is irrelevant. These days, our biggest competition in the market is artificial intelligence, not other traders or institutions. The robots are real, and they don't get emotional – let that be our inspiration!

(j) Market cheerleaders

A can-do attitude is desirable in corporate circles, because the worst crime in the boardroom is to be perceived as 'negative,' but traders must remain neutrally pragmatic in their outlook. Being 'passionate' about our chosen profession looks great on a résumé, but in the markets everything is not awesome and there are many things which can't be done.

There comes a time when we realize we have to stop going to 21st birthday parties. Likewise, when we mature as traders, the hype, glitter and flashing lights of the market lose their appeal. When we trade, we will have good days and bad days, but they all come and go and we realize over time there is nothing to get overly excited about. When we engage with the market, we should do so from the perspective of a political attaché – not a cheerleader.

(k) No winning, no losing

Strictly speaking, we don't have 'winning' or 'losing' trades: we have trades which increase or decrease the balance in our account. Winning implies we have defeated someone or something; it implies our gain is more than financial. It never is. Likewise, losing is associated with losers, something we never want to be. Yet the best traders are the ones who know how to lose well.

The concept of winning and losing helps to explain the process of trading for many of us, but we should be mindful of this type of language creeping into our trading vocabulary. We shouldn't take things literally and we should always remember we are talking about so-called 'winning and losing.'

If we become attached to the feeling of winning and recoil from the sensation of losing, we will always be upset even when our trading is profitable. A profitable day trading strategy can 'lose' money about 30–40% of the time. Swing trading will take a negative hit on 40–50%

of occasions, while weekly position trading can incur a loss up to 60% of the time. These strategies can be 'losing' most of the time, but they still remain profitable over the long run.

(l) Smartphones

For many of us, our smartphone has become a digital pacifier which we instinctively reach for when an anxious thought arises. We don't need to know every market event as it happens, just as we don't need to constantly monitor our pulse to know we are still alive.

If we're continually checking the market it can feel like we're truly on top of things, but we're just subjecting ourselves to a deluge of distraction and frustration. Considering the temperament of the market, do we really want her whispering in our ear 24/7? Traders need to be smarter than their phone and put a limit on their market interaction.

(m) Trading short

As any double agent will tell you, things get complicated when you're playing both sides.

Shorting stocks sounds like a great idea and short sellers are the stuff of legend. But the practice is not without its drawbacks. Short trades carry significantly more risk because we are at the mercy of the market from the get-go and she is not known for her charity.

When we short a stock, our broker borrows shares from other clients on our behalf and immediately sells them into the market for us. We do this because we believe the share price is about to drop and we plan to buy them back later at a cheaper price to settle our debt. This all takes place behind the scenes in a split second and all we have to do is press a button. Then, when the time comes to settle our debts, we 'buy to cover' our liabilities.

When a short trade works out, it can be spectacular because it produces a significant profit very quickly. They say the market climbs up the stairs, step by step, but comes down in the elevator. In a severe crash, it dispenses with the elevator and jumps out the window. If we can short the market as it begins its downward trajectory, we will do very well for ourselves.

A market correction gets coverage in the mainstream media and everyone starts fretting about stocks. If we're sitting pretty in a short position we can feel very clever, but we must never get complacent as short trades should be true to their name and have a very limited lifespan.

There are four reasons for this:

1. Trading on the short side is likely to be a counter-trend trade because the long-term equity market trend is up. Unless the stock we are shorting is in terminal decline, when the current correction ends, the equity market will recover and go on to make new highs. This means a short trade is like walking backwards in the market and we're constantly looking over our shoulder.

2. A trader holding a short position has a liability for shares he doesn't own. At some point in the future he has to go to the open market to get shares to settle his debt. The shares he originally sold aren't held in escrow, he must buy new shares at the prevailing rate – which is determined by the prevailing mood. When the market is rising, and sellers are holding out for higher prices, buyers are forced to pay up – they can't stand aside.

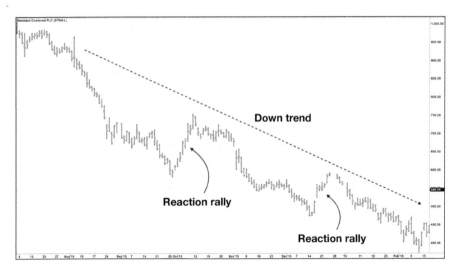

FIGURE 10: DAILY BAR CHART OF STANDARD CHARTERED (STAN.L) SHOWING REACTION RALLIES IN A DOWN TREND

A successful short trade is like a loan from a regulated bank which is partially written off by an abrupt devaluation of the stock price. When a short trade goes against us, it's as if the bank sells the loan to the mob and they squeeze us for more than the original amount – and they want it all paid now.

A **short squeeze** occurs when all the loans are called in at once and the panicking buyers flood the market with frantic buy orders. Trading against a short squeeze (taking advantage of the mob's victims) is a highly profitable trading strategy.

For this reason, the market can rally strongly after a sudden sell off. This 'reaction rally' is driven by optimism among buyers and relief that the correction may be over – but it's usually magnified by a short squeeze.

3. When we trade a long position, we have more control because we're holding an asset and can only lose what's in our account. In a short trade, we are carrying an unknown liability and our eventual loss can exceed our account balance. Accordingly, when you read the fine print in your broker's terms and conditions, you notice they

reserve the right to intervene in our short trades and close out our positions at any time.

4. The profits from long trades are compounded, whereas the profits from short trades are amortized. Compounding is when we are making profit on top of profit and there is no upper limit to the potential gain. Amortization is the opposite: the longer it goes on, the less we can make. As the stock we are shorting continues to drop, the pie keeps shrinking, so our ability to profit from it keeps reducing – it's the law of diminishing returns.

(n) Health

Not surprisingly, traders do a lot of sitting around. The plus side of this is that they can be sitting anywhere in the world. The downside is posture and back problems, not to mention a fat belly. Various professional traders have come up with novel ideas to address the issue, such as taking frequent breaks or working on a treadmill. Whatever solution we devise, we need to be mindful of our physical health, as the lack of exercise associated with trading takes a toll.

The popular image of guys in colorful numbered jackets shouting at each other in the pit is far removed from the daily experience of private traders. Trading, if done properly, is actually a low-key process. Traders are usually on their own in a rented office or at home, as they go through their daily routine. Good traders tend to be individual in their thinking and social habits, so they don't have an issue with periods of solitary confinement.

For this reason, private traders need to be grounded and centered because the job can have a serious impact on mental health, especially if a trader is prone to stress or anxiety. The best traders know their mind and don't allow themselves to fall into a rut or spiral downwards following a series of losses. They don't overthink things and regularly give their body and mind a break by engaging in physical activities totally unrelated to trading.

(o) Good news

When it comes to macroeconomics (the big picture), I believe there is no better source of information than *The Economist*. It provides insightful and understandable analysis of global economics and politics. In addition, this publication is not afraid to challenge conventional thinking and vested interests head on. A survey of 8,728 Americans in March 2017 by Michael W. Kearney of the University of Missouri, found *The Economist* to be the most trusted news source in the U.S.[5]

In a world of 'alternative facts', we have to pay for the truth. As traders and investors, we should commit to reading this publication from cover to cover every single week. Surprisingly, for such a widely-read publication, it's very good at identifying new social trends and opportunities which can be profitably traded using long-term strategies.

As private traders we have to keep overheads to a minimum, so free sources of information on the web are always welcome. However, there is a trade-off because we can't honestly expect to get intelligent and in-depth market analysis on an ongoing basis for free. Sure, we will find snippets here and there, but good analysis takes time and that also has a cost.

(p) End-of-days

Before charting and technical analysis was widely available on PCs, traders would use just seven numbers (time, date, open, high, low, close and volume) to manually draw charts and indicators on graph paper. This was a laborious task, but everything grew from these seed numbers and it gave traders a wonderful feel for the market. When

---

5   *Trusting News Project Report 2017*, A Reynolds Journalism Institute research project, Michael W. Kearney, 25 July 2017 (www.rjionline.org/reporthtml.html).

the price exploded upwards or collapsed downwards, it would literally go off the chart and they would have to start again with a new sheet of paper and adjust the scale.

When they had to draw four or five lines which were 10–15mm high and then the next four lines were 3–4mm high, they physically felt the price compressing and the volatility changing. They knew the market could be topping out or pausing before striding higher because they documented the change themselves, rather than having it presented to them.

As we dump a ton of technical indicators on a chart we are subjecting ourselves to too much information, and the simple but profound message of price action contained in the seven numbers is lost. When beginners rely totally on pre-generated indicators and charts they can literally lose the plot.

I am not suggesting we dust off the graph paper and coloring pencils, but I firmly believe we can gain a valuable insight into the markets when we source our own data for charting. Few traders do this, and I believe a wonderful advantage can be gained by the process.

All we need is some charting software which allows the import of third party data. There is no need to concern ourselves with overly complex metadata, as historical end-of-day (EOD) data is freely available on the web in comma separated value (.csv) file formats.

CSV files are a delight to work with and a reminder of days when computers were used to compute. Each row on the file is a separate data record, which in our case will be the seven seed numbers of a price bar. When viewed in a text document format, the values are separated by a comma – hence the name.

The EOD data required to plot a week's worth of daily price bars on a chart (excluding time) looks like this:

Date, Open, High, Low, Close, Volume

03/06/17, 125.12, 132.21, 120.63, 123.29, 365040

03/07/17, 124.15, 131.96, 119.34, 122.75, 330102

03/08/17, 100.97, 122.18, 100.31, 121.13, 359862

03/09/17, 115.01, 122.39, 113.45, 118.82, 455932

03/10/17, 117.32, 118.34, 100.42, 117.94, 387651

To make the exercise interesting and potentially profitable, we might want to develop our own indicator or index. It doesn't have to be complicated because we can work with a closing price. In this case, we just need 'Date' and 'Close' in the header row.

Our index might be based on advancing and declining stocks, IPOs in a month, social media mentions or even electricity consumption (a great indicator of activity in the 'real economy'). The purpose of the exercise is to gain a perspective on internal market activity which we feel is not being examined by others.

When we work exclusively with pre-prepared indicators and data it's like getting a take-out meal every night. The food is OK, but we must eat what's on the menu and so does everyone else. Making the effort to get our own data and create indicators is like sourcing natural ingredients and learning to cook for ourselves. Apart from the financial health benefits, we gain independence from others and a deeper understanding of the market environment.

(q) Post-truth trading

Recently, social media shacked up with propaganda and gave birth to the terrible twins of 'fake news' and 'post-truth'. Back in the day, duping the public was more difficult because the lies had to make sense, otherwise no one would believe them. That doesn't appear to be an issue anymore.

The 'post-truth' phenomenon came as a surprise to many and was proclaimed word of the year in 2016.[6] It's defined as, "Relating to or denoting circumstances in which objective facts are less influential in shaping public opinion than appeals to emotion and personal belief."

That also happens to be a perfect definition of the market. Accordingly, post-truth came as no surprise to experienced traders, because they already operate in the ultimate post-truth environment.

(1) Trade ideas

Trying to trade someone else's ideas is like trying to comb our hair while looking at their reflection. Ultimately, we are our own opponent when we trade, so mimicking the actions of others is pointless. As we saw earlier, the best trading coaches show us how to trade but don't spoon feed us setups.

We should never compare our performance to others or assume we will have the same results by following them. We will only progress as traders when we can analyze the market ourselves, formulate trade plans based on that analysis and implement those ideas in accordance with our rules. This is probably the most valuable lesson I learned.

4. Routine

A sure sign our revival is gathering steam is when we fall into a trading routine – we already looked at the importance of this in the previous chapter. However, it's one thing to understand the need for a routine, and another thing entirely to have one and use it consistently.

Inconsistency with our approach to the market and a lack of routine is another hurdle we create for ourselves. This is not unique to trading and manifests in all areas of life, as we keep changing our mind and

---

6   Oxford Dictionaries (en.oxforddictionaries.com/definition/post-truth).

dropping opinions we previously held. How many times have we looked at old photos of ourselves and smiled at the naivety of the clothes we were wearing or the things we were up to at the time? Will the future 'us' be smiling when we look back on what we are doing in the market right now?

Just because something is new and different doesn't make it better. Inconsistency is lethal in trading because we keep jumping from one strategy and style to the next without ever mastering one of them. It's not a case of 'This time, it's different' – it's more a case of this time, we're different. We are always different and that's the problem. We keep changing our views on the market, our perception of how to trade it and our belief in where the profit lies. We lack consistency in our thinking and longevity in our methods.

Regardless of how we feel or what's going on in the world, we have to keep plugging away at our strategies and going through our daily trading chores. As they say, 'If you're not in, you can't win' – and in the market some of the biggest wins are when few people are in. By sticking to a routine, traders will be in the market when it offers the greatest returns.

The Wall Street recovery

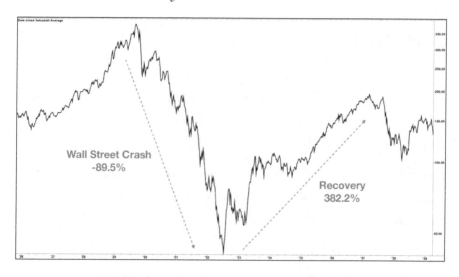

FIGURE 11: DOW JONES INDUSTRIAL AVERAGE (1926–1939)

The famous Wall Street Crash which began in September 1929 and bottomed out three years later, with the Dow Jones Industrial Average losing 89.5% in the process, is firmly engraved in financial history. Surprisingly, we never hear about the fantastic Wall Street recovery which followed. From the bottom in July 1932 until March 1937, the Dow recovered strongly and gained 382.2% over five years, in the midst of the 'Great Depression'.

FIGURE 12: S&P 500 (2006–2018)

A more recent example followed the crash of 2008. To this day, I meet people who got burned and swear they will never touch shares again – what a pity. The S&P 500 hit the floor on 6 March 2009 having lost 57%, but gained over 340% in the following nine years when it reached 2940.91 in September 2018.

5. Reward

Having learned to control our losses, the profits will look after themselves. The most important thing here is to trust our strategy and concentrate on the routine. We should not count the money when trading and it's a good idea to minimize the window on our trading platform which displays our account balance.

When we have a few positions open during the day, we shouldn't really know how much we are up or down in cash terms. Profit in trading is like grass on the front lawn. If we start measuring it, it will never grow because we are standing on it and blocking the sunlight. But if we concentrate on maintaining our tools and using good fertilizer, soon enough we will be up to our ankles in the green stuff.

Very few of us need advice on how to spend money, but if we can roll up our profits rather than spending them, we can slowly shift into longer-term investments. If we are not making a profit and short-term trading isn't working out for us, there is no reason we can't use the experience gained to manage an investment portfolio. In this way, the time we spent learning the markets will not go to waste.

SIX EDGES

The Psychological Tools of a Successful Trader

HAVING EXAMINED THE path a trader must follow, we will now look closely at the six psychological tools which facilitate the journey.

No box

Beginners assume they need a secret strategy to be successful. This is an attractive narrative, because the majority of traders lose money, so the elite minority must have an 'edge' which sets them apart. The quest for this elusive edge is just a distraction from the more important things traders should be doing and exposes them to exploitation by snake oil merchants.

Thinking we can get an edge somewhere is like the silly management cliché that we should, 'Think outside the box.' There is no box – there never has been. The belief in a box outside of which we must think actually fashions one from our ego and places us inside it, because it makes us believe our perspective is unique. We are like a busload of tourists who all buy the same t-shirt. Each believes they are different because they got their name printed on it, yet the store owner keeps all the t-shirts in the same box beside the printer.

Head office

Other traders are exactly like us. They believe (as we do) that they have an edge. This is in spite of the fact that we are all using the same software, reading the same books and probably attending the same courses too. They are looking at the same screens as us and their eyes and brains are just as effective as ours. In fact, the person on the opposite side of our trade might as well be us, because there is very little difference between us.

Therefore, the only way to get ahead in the market (to triumph over ourselves), is to act in a manner which is out of character for traders and do things we don't think we should be doing. To facilitate that, we need to get to the root of our actions and go to our head office.

A science of the mind

We have all encountered business gurus, life coaches and motivation experts. These people use various techniques to help us replace negative and destructive thoughts and habits with positive and constructive thoughts and actions. This concept of working directly with our mind to effect change in our life is a relatively new phenomenon in the West but has been widely practiced in the East for countless generations.

In my experience, Tibetan Buddhists are way ahead of the curve on this. Often referred to as 'A Science of the Mind,' this tradition has specialized in transforming and training minds for over 1,400 years. A lot has changed in that time, but our thoughts and emotions still work exactly the same. There is a robust tradition of analysis on the

Himalayan Plateau where everything (and I mean everything) is examined in the search for understanding.

In the Far East, Tibetan Buddhism is sometimes perceived as complex and mysterious. In the Far West, it's often seen as a flaky philosophy for hibernating hippies and liberal yuppies. I'm not so sure about all that, because the Middle Way contains the most pragmatic methods for working with our mind that I have ever encountered.

In fact, many western psychotherapy techniques in common use today have similarities with long-established methods for transforming the mind found in The Middle Kingdom. Techniques such as cognitive behavioral therapy, visualization and many other self-awareness practices spring to mind. Even the 12-step program, used so successfully to treat addiction, bears a striking resemblance to the ancient Tibetan practice of Ngöndro.

The Six Paramitas

A perfect example of this is mindfulness. Personal development professionals and therapists have recently embraced the practice and every self-respecting course now has a module on mindfulness. This is wonderful, because any attempt to free our mind from endless distraction will ultimately be beneficial, regardless of our motivation.

But mindfulness is just the tip of the iceberg. The pathways of the Himalayas are paved with countless practical methods for working with our mind, such as 'The Seven Points of Mind Training' and 'The Eight Verses for Training the Mind'. While all of these are essential to make any sort of meaningful progress in life, we are going to explore how 'The Six Paramitas' can be used to transform our approach to trading.

Paramita is a Sanskrit word which translates rather grandly into English as 'transcendent action' or 'transcendent perfection'. We don't need to go out and buy an edge, because we already have six of them. We just need to realize their potential, sharpen them up and apply them to our trading. The Paramitas are: generosity, discipline, patience, diligence, concentration and wisdom.

1. Generosity

Generosity is generally understood in terms of giving things away, such as our possessions or our time. But it's really about "cultivating the attitude of generosity." Far too often, we give to others and expect appreciation in return. In these situations, we are not really giving, we are bargaining – our generosity comes with a price. To properly embrace generosity, we must give and expect nothing back. If we feel resentful after we have given something and not received thanks, this is a sure sign we lack the attitude of generosity.

In terms of trading, we must be prepared to give up our time freely and not expect a reward for every minute we spend in front of the screen. We are not consultants or taxi drivers; we can't bill the market by the hour. We must be prepared to spend days, weeks and even months trading the markets and expect nothing in return.

A MONEY-BACK GUARANTEE

Not only have we to surrender our time, we also have to give money to the market by opening our account and embracing the risk. Our cash won't grow if it's locked away in the dark and sterile environment of our broker's safe. This is especially relevant after a loss. If our strategy is flagging entry signals, we must be generous with our cash because these occasions are when we can make a year's wages in a short period of time.

The market abounds with irony, but one of the greatest of these is that we must forget about making money in an environment which appears to exist for that sole purpose. Trading is not about counting pennies or pining after the money we have sitting in the market. We are either a trader or an accountant; we can't be both. When we concentrate on the art of trading and generously open our account to the market, the profits will flow as a matter of course.

Besides, as our skills and experience grow, we are creating a money-back guarantee.

2. Discipline

This is an interesting one. For many of us discipline is about restriction or denial. We are forcing ourselves to do the 'right thing' even though the 'wrong thing' feels so good. The image that frequently springs to mind is a school headmaster, a drill sergeant or an economist at the IMF – somebody imposing the law on us or telling us what to do.

In the ancient texts, discipline is described as "appropriate action." This is a very different approach to how we usually perceive discipline. It tells us we should see it in terms of what we should do, rather than what we should not do. Discipline is not about suppressing or controlling something, it's about doing the appropriate thing at a given point in time.

We need to be a little careful with this one, because discipline for its own sake is pointless and potentially dangerous. We can be very hard on ourselves when we trade, especially if we are ambitious by nature. We shouldn't set impossible goals and expect to be highly profitable from the get-go, because the process will take time. We should cut ourselves some slack.

WHAT IS DISCIPLINE IN TRADING?

Discipline in trading means sticking to the plan because we know it will keep us out of trouble and in the profit zone. It means not acting on impulse but waiting for our entry triggers to occur because we know all good trades begin that way. It's about placing our protective stop every time we open a position because we know we will forget it later.

It's about going through our daily pre-trading checklist because we know from past experience if we enter the market unprepared we will be punished. It's about doing our analysis and preparation on the weekend when everyone else is at the ball game. It's about entering the trade when we are supposed to, even though it looks scary, because we failed to do that in the past and kicked ourselves afterwards.

MINDLESS MARKET-WATCHING

We also need to apply discipline to the time we spend in front of the screen. We must be generous with the time we give to trading, but this needs to be done in a balanced way. If we are not careful, we can spend hours staring at charts, mindlessly watching the market. Instead, we should set an alert or conditional order for our favorite trading setup and leave the screen.

A GOOD FRIEND

In short, discipline is about doing the right thing at the right time because experience has taught us that is the most profitable thing to do. Discipline is not a burden like a heavy chain tying us down and preventing us from going somewhere. It's a benefit, like a good friend who keeps us out of sticky situations, and puts us in touch with profitable trading opportunities.

3. Patience

This is described as, "The ability not to be perturbed or upset by anything." Again, a very different perspective. It shows us that patience is not about waiting around for something to happen or biding our time. It's more to do with personal contentment. When we are content with our lot, patience is a natural by-product of our experience. It's not that we 'have' patience, it's more like we don't have distress. If we have a stressed, anxious or unsettled mind then we will not possess the foundation from which patience arises.

Just like generosity, patience should not be connected to a reward. It's not about putting up with something for a period and then we get the pay-off. True patience is not conditional upon an end to the situation requiring its use. We should have patience regardless of the outcome because sometimes the situation requiring patience can last our entire life.

A TEST OF PATIENCE

We all have patience to some degree, but we only discover how much when it's tested. The market is eminently qualified to perform that test. If we are unable to wait ten minutes for the next subway train or the lady searching for pennies in the supermarket line, how likely are we to sit in a profitable trade for weeks or months?

Before we trade cash in the market, we need to bring order to our life, because the market will do everything possible to perturb and upset us. In this regard, the market is like a discount airline; the less baggage we are carrying, the cheaper and less stressful the journey will be.

In practical terms, patience means we have to stay away from our trading account during our 'risk off' periods. This is when the market is not conducive to our trading style. We need to sit back and wait for the market to come to us, rather than chasing after it. We also need to be able to stay in a position when our indicators are telling us everything is fine, but our mind and the market gurus are telling us the opposite.

WAITING IN THE EMERGENCY DEPARTMENT

We need to experience difficult trades many times before the importance of patience begins to dawn on us. How often have we been impatient to jump into a trade only to see the price sit there doing nothing for days after we enter? Eagerness to trade is like an ambulance that rushes to the scene of an accident, only to bring the patient to the emergency department where he spends hours waiting on a stretcher to see the doctor.

Patience has always been important for traders, but I believe it will offer a huge advantage in future. Older people always bemoan the fact that the young have no patience, but this generation of pensioners might actually be right. For the first time in history, a society is emerging where people have come to expect immediate answers and instant gratification. Thanks to Google and online retailers, we are getting both! In the not-too-distant future, traders with abundant patience will stand out from the market crowd like never before.

PLAYING THE HARP

Making money from the market is a bit like making money from playing the harp. Learning the harp requires dedication and study over many years; having some talent is also helpful. Learning to play the market is even more demanding, because it's constantly playing us too.

If we are serious about trading, we need to slow down and give the process time. One of the great ironies of the trading game is that the market is frantic, furious and complex, yet the people who trade it profitably are relaxed, steady and simple in their outlook. If we concentrate on learning the ropes and improving our skills, the rewards will come in time. To succeed as traders we need patience, because the market has none.

A PERSONAL PATIENCE COACH

Frustration at the market is common among beginners. Left unchecked it will eventually lead to anger. This in turn leads to uncontrolled trading, which will undoubtedly lead to losses. Patience is the antidote to anger because it addresses frustration at its source. As traders, we must train ourselves in patience at all times. There are a number of ways to do this.

One particularly useful method is to imagine the market mistress is also a personal patience coach. Apart from providing us with a living, she is going to train us in patience as well. Best of all, she is kind enough to do it for free! She has studied us very closely and knows exactly the right buttons to push and doesn't hold back. Like all good coaches, she is constantly setting exercises and tests for us in many ingenious ways. We need to realize everything that provokes and upsets us when trading is just another one of her thoughtful exercises.

The market constantly provides opportunities to train in patience, and in so doing it hands us a tool to make profit – if only we realize it. If we adopt this attitude, not only will we cultivate enormous patience over time, but we will find it hard not to laugh when faced with recurring challenges.

Standing aside

Standing aside is a valid trading position, and the only one in which you cannot suffer a loss. It is also the best way to preserve the capital in our trading account. The most profitable traders have excellent patience and often stay out of the market for long periods waiting for the correct conditions to set up.

Fear of missing out (FOMO) causes countless traders to jump into a sharply rising market just as it is about to change direction. In the process, they buy overpriced shares from professionals who then stand aside and wait for the next opportunity.

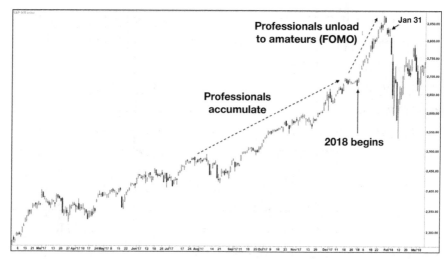

FIGURE 13: DAILY CHART OF THE S&P 500 (MARCH 2017–MARCH 2018)

For example, in January 2018, the U.S. market exploded upwards into a parabolic climb as retail traders and investors poured into equities fearing they would miss out on another year of record gains. In the process, many professional traders I spoke to took profits as they unloaded the positions they had accumulated in the latter stages of 2017. This mass transference of risk continued for the entire month of January.

As if on cue, the last day of January saw the beginning of a correction and the market fell by 11.8% before it bottomed out on 9 February, in the process inflicting significant losses on impatient amateur traders.

4. Diligence

The conventional definition of diligence is, "Constant and earnest effort to accomplish what is undertaken."[1] In the Paramitas, it is defined as, "To find joy in what is virtuous, positive and wholesome." Note how the regular description emphasizes the activity, whereas the Paramita approach focuses on the mental attitude.

---

1   www.thefreedictionary.com

In Buddhist traditions, the Six Paramitas are used to train the mind in compassion. Everyone who knows me will confirm I know nothing about that, but I can imagine it must be very difficult to remain diligently compassionate in the world of today. Anyone who manages to accomplish that must be on to something. It would appear they realized long ago that the key to diligence is inspiration. The emphasis needs to be on finding joy in what we are doing rather than just getting on with it.

Unless we enjoy an activity, sooner or later we will give up. This ties in with the idea that if we love our job, we will never have to work a day in our life. If we are to maintain constant and earnest effort in our trading, we need to find joy in it. So how do we do that if we are demoralized by constant losses and frustrated by the market?

BE INSPIRED

We need to realize what inspires us and what demotivates us. We need to recognize the things which stress us out, and appreciate the things which give us a boost. For example, I like to have at least one weekly position trade open most of the time because it feels like I am always ahead. A swing trade might produce the same amount of profit in a few days, but it doesn't last very long. Likewise, a day trade might be very profitable, but it's over and done in a few hours.

At the end of the year when we review our account, all three styles might be equally profitable. But swing and day trades produce lumps of money in short bursts, whereas weekly trend following gives a steady and reassuring trickle of funds all the time. Each month the profit from a weekly position trade might be small, but it can be very beneficial on a psychological level.

A VEGETARIAN LION

We can also draw inspiration from nature. A few years ago, my sister and her husband went on a safari to the Maasai Mara in Kenya. As they were recalling their adventures, I was surprised to learn that a lion is successful less than one time in five when he hunts alone. But the lion never gives up, because he is a lion and that's what he does. He would never dream of questioning his hunting strategies or himself. Yet, despite having a success rate of less than 20%, the lion remains at the top of the food chain.

Bear in mind, trading is part of the financial services industry, so terms and conditions apply to everything – including animal metaphors. Let's not get too inspired by the lion's diligence because there is one key difference between us. The lion must keep hunting in order to survive. Eventually he will starve if he doesn't catch something. As his hunger grows, he will take greater risks by attacking fitter and stronger prey. We, on the other hand, never have to trade – the vegetarian option is always on the table.

STARVING TO TRADE

Trading can be a bit of a drag, especially when things aren't going well. But we need to figure out how to make it interesting and find joy in the constant and earnest effort of following our strategy, rather than the act of making money. If the effort is attached to the money rather than the process, we will start taking unnecessary risks or overtrade during unsuitable conditions because we feel we are starving.

A trader who diligently grabs a few per cent all the time, will make a decent living from the market for as long as he wishes. Traders constantly chasing huge gains will get them occasionally, but will blow out their account sooner or later – it's just a matter of time.

5. Concentration (mindfulness)

Blaise Pascal was a mathematician, physicist, inventor and philosopher.[2] Born in France, 21 years after the first stock exchange opened, he was a child prodigy and was educated by his father, a tax collector. Among

---

2   Bernstein, Peter, *Against the Gods: The Remarkable Story of Risk*, 1998, Wiley, ISBN-13: 978-0471295631.

traders, Pascal is known as a pioneer of **probability theory** and is said to have invented a roulette wheel. Less well known is the fact that he told us, "All of humanity's problems stem from man's inability to sit quietly in a room alone."

Endless conceptual thinking and distraction are what prevent us from sitting quietly. It's unbelievable how much of our time is wasted every day on mental gossip and the constant activity it inspires. As we jump from one idea to the next, one topic to another, our mind is everywhere except where it is supposed to be. One Tibetan teacher describes this as "monkey mind," because our mind is constantly hopping from one subject to the next and never settles.

It's amazing to think Pascal recognized this almost 400 years ago. Even more incredible, the Buddha identified the exact same issue over 2,000 years before that, and thought many different methods to address it. But here we are today, still struggling with the exact same problem. In the language of Pascal, *"Plus ça change, plus c'est la même chose."*[3]

DOING NOTHING

Most of us fill our lives with constant activity to keep our mind busy. How many books have we read and how many movies have we watched because we had to give our mind something to do? It's as if we are afraid to be quiet and alone for fear of what might happen. We feel we might fall into depression or we're wasting our life by sitting on our ass being 'unproductive'.

Mindfulness cuts through this misconception because it allows us to be at peace with ourselves and the world around us without doing anything. After all, we are human beings, not human doings. We should be content simply to be, rather than constantly looking for something to do. Mindfulness allows our mind to rest in its natural state of peace and clarity – any other state of mind is unnatural.

---

3   "The more things change, the more they stay the same."

DEGREES OF MINDFULNESS

We shouldn't be put off mindfulness just because it's currently popular with trendy New Age types. Over the centuries, it has fallen in and out of fashion. In fact, various forms of mindfulness are found in cultures throughout the world. Frequently it is integrated with spiritual practice such as prayer or mantra recitation. It can also be found in martial arts and traditional dance where movement is used as a method of concentration.

We all practice a degree of mindfulness when we make a conscious and deliberate effort to focus on what we are doing at any given time. This might be in a work environment when we are engaged in an important project, or even when we take part in a sports activity.

Mindfulness happens on many levels, but **concentration meditation** is a more formal practice where we deliberately place our attention lightly on an object. In so doing, it allows our mind to settle and enter a state of non-distraction.

Traditionally our breath is used as the object of focus because its energy is closely connected to the mind and it's always with us. When we are comfortable focusing on our breath, we can experiment with other things such as sound, sight or sensation. When our practice is more stable, we can start to use thoughts and emotions as our object of focus – and that's when things really get interesting!

The main thing is to slow down and concentrate on the object of our practice, without fixating on it. In order to do this, we need to let go of discursive thinking. Realizing we are engaged in mental gossip, and bringing our attention back to our object of focus, is the key to the practice. By repeatedly letting go of thoughts, we slowly weaken the mind's habit of grasping at them and creating 'after thoughts' which lead to further distraction.

Applying ourselves to the **method**, rather than the desired result, is the key to mindfulness practice. It is also the key to profitable trading! When we devote ourselves to the process, the result we are seeking naturally arises – almost as a side effect. In mindfulness, it is presence and peace – in trading, it's profit. This is not immediately obvious to beginners, because the process and the outcome they seek appear unconnected.

BENEFITS OF MINDFULNESS

Numerous recent scientific studies have confirmed the benefits of mindfulness – benefits which practitioners have known about for millennia. Obviously meditation is not a substitute for medication, but mindfulness increases concentration while reducing stress and anxiety. It also improves our ability to relate to others and is an excellent method for dealing with impulsive behavior. Most importantly, it centers us by bringing stability, calmness and grounding to everything we do.

When we sit mindfully, we experience contentment based on an acceptance of the reality of our situation, rather than the usual short-term escapist distractions and projects we pursue. This is exactly the mindset we need to operate in a fluid and nonsensical environment like the market.

ATTACHMENT AND AVERSION

Another benefit of mindfulness is learning to deal with feelings of **attachment** and **aversion**. This means letting go of pleasant things we are attached to and accepting unpleasant things we have an aversion to. This is important because attachment and aversion are two of the root causes of suffering in life. Everything keeps changing and sooner or later we lose everything we are attached to – while getting the things we have an aversion to.

We have attachment and aversion to people, places and objects, but also to thoughts and emotions and concepts of how the world should be and our place in it. Traders need to be acutely aware of this, because attachment to winning trades (and feeling like a winner) and aversion to losing trades (and feeling like a loser) is the main cause of suffering for us.

MINDFULNESS IN TRADING

If we break the law, we're sent to prison. If we break the rules in prison, we're put in solitary confinement. The prison authorities use our untamed 'monkey mind' against us as the highest form of punishment. And that's exactly what the market does too! When we practice mindfulness, the monkey dissolves and we remove the power the market has over us.

Therefore, to derive the maximum benefit from mindfulness, we need to integrate the practice into our trading. It's all very well being mindful for a few minutes in our apartment in the morning, but when the shit hits the fan in the market, that's when we really need it.

As traders, we are already sitting down, so we might as well do a mindfulness practice. It doesn't have to be anything formal. We can begin by mindfully drinking a cup of tea or entering orders and allowing that to evolve into a short practice. The secret is to just start doing it and not to worry about doing it right or wrong.

It's impossible to describe meditation in writing without giving rise to endless questions and concepts. The notion of 'letting go of thoughts' is alien to most of us and even fanciful for some. It's hard to explain, it has to be experienced to be understood – just try it!

MEASURE TWICE, CUT ONCE

When we trade, we are always on a tide, "which taken at the flood, leads on to fortune". Things happen very quickly in a flood and it is of vital importance that we are not distracted when entering orders or making trading decisions. Trading should be conducted with the same level of concentration and organization we apply when booking an important flight.

We need to be fully present and aware – if not, we will pay a hefty price for our lack of concentration. We should ensure there are no unnecessary interruptions, get the trade booked and then leave it. If we are interspersing our trading with other activities, sooner or later it will cost us.

To address the issue, we should use a two-stage order entry process. As carpenters like to say, 'measure twice and cut once.' First, we create and enter the order, then a pop-up window should summarize the order and ask us if we wish to proceed. We should train ourselves to count to five at this point and only then confirm the order is right.

Sitting practice

It's imperative we make a conscious effort to be mindful before we trade. The first item of the **Eight Checks** (page 147) is 'myself', where we do a brief mindfulness practice, followed by an analysis of our current experience. It's amazing how our mood and concentration levels can change by sitting quietly for a few minutes and observing our mind.

Jesse Livermore told us it was his sitting that made him the big money. That's reassuring, because mindfulness is traditionally known as 'sitting practice'.

6. Wisdom

Wisdom brings the other five Paramitas together, so they work as one, like the fingers on our hand. Wisdom is described as, "The perfect discernment of all knowable things." A proper explanation of that is beyond the ability of this writer, because in this context it involves a profound insight into the nature of reality and the nature of mind (I'm told they're the same thing).

My limited understanding of the subject extends to a vague realization that very little of what we perceive truly is as it appears. The financial markets are a reflection of society and we know society is rarely what it appears to be on the surface – so that's a great place to start.

Whether we are aware of it or not, almost everything we do in life is driven by the pursuit of happiness and the avoidance of suffering. We see happiness as a beautiful but illusive butterfly, so we chase after it. At the same time, we see suffering as a hungry wolf nipping at our heels. If we stopped running and sat for a while, we would realize the wolf's bark is worse than his bite and he is only playing with the butterfly. To be happy, we just need to get out of their way.

When we realize everyone else is engaged in the same illusory chase and we view the economic impact of the process in the markets – no wonder they don't make sense!

DISCONTENTMENT AND TRADING

For a capitalist society to function, people must spend vast amounts of time and money chasing their butterflies and avoiding their wolves. Discontentment is the engine that drives consumer society. We must keep buying stuff to keep the whole thing going around.

For as long as human beings have been able to think, the wisdom teachers and philosophers of many traditions and cultures have been telling us the same thing. Namely, all the happiness we could ever want in life is already present within us. We don't have to acquire tons of stuff or achieve 'great things' such as climb mountains, run marathons or build business empires.

In spite of this (or maybe because of it), billions of dollars are spent on consumer advertising every year, all of which perpetuates a lack of contentment in us. When we enter the market, we bring our discontentment with us and it can have a profoundly negative effect on our account balance.

NOT ANOTHER PROJECT

Apart from constantly buying crap we don't need, we also go from one project to another as our life unfolds. Trading should not be just another project, because trading will not make us happy. If anything, it will make happiness more elusive as our frustration and confusion grows, so we must never allow trading to become a proxy for happiness.

Rather than chasing an elusive fortune in the markets, we should be content to make a decent return on our capital and accept when we have enough. As Pascal might have put it, 'Ça suffit!'[4]

For this reason, we need to be crystal clear why we are trading. I know traders who are very wealthy and don't need more money, yet they continue to trade. They need to do something to pass the day and give them a reason to get out of bed in the morning. Managing a trading account is a lot easier than restoring a vintage car. These traders are very clear about their reason for being in the market – are you?

THE GURU MARKET

Guru is another Sanskrit word and it means a 'teacher or a guide.' In contemporary English, it can have a slight derogatory meaning and is often used to describe a charlatan or a self-proclaimed expert. Market gurus are plentiful and a great source of debate, most of which should be consumed with a liberal pinch of salt. Professional traders find gurus highly entertaining (unless they are one) and tend to ignore them.

We don't need a market guru to interpret things for us, because the market itself is one of the best teachers we will ever encounter. Apart from our own body, I can think of no better example of interdependence and impermanence. An understanding of these two goes to the very heart of what market wisdom is about.

---

4   'That's enough!'

Interdependence means everything, and everyone is connected and dependent on everything else – there is no such thing as 'individual'. We see this all the time where an announcement in one part of the world immediately impacts stocks on another continent. In the markets, nothing unfolds in a vacuum – it's all interconnected. A stock, commodity or currency pair depends on a very specific set of causes and conditions being present to move. Interdependence drives the market.

Impermanence is a bit more challenging to contemplate, because it's often only understood in terms of death. This subject is the ultimate taboo in modern society. Nobody wants to talk about death because we feel to do so would invite it into our life. Contemplation of death forces us to ponder the relevance of everything we do. It also undermines most of the pillars on which our lives are built.

More importantly it raises the question of which part of us (if any) will continue after death, where is it now and where was it before we were born? It never ceases to amaze me how we spend most of our adult life contributing to a pension fund we might never get to use, yet we pay scant attention to the eternity that is guaranteed to follow our death. That's a profound failure of risk assessment – especially for traders who claim to be pragmatic!

CHANGE

Impermanence isn't only about death, it's about change. Without impermanence, there would be no trading. Traders seek out beginnings and endings – volatility and movement. The transient nature of the market puts food on our table. It's about the constant cycle of birth and death in the market.

For a new trend to form, the previous one has to end. The birth of the bull can only take place when the bear has passed away. Firms are born in the market with an IPO and die when they go bust or get taken over. Traders are midwives and undertakers to the market, the never-ending wheel of birth and death on the exchanges keeps them in a job.

SOCRATES IN SPACE

Popular culture has elevated wisdom to a distant cliché. Its ambassador is the little green guy in *Star Wars* or the broken warrior who 'finds himself' in a mountain-top temple and returns to inflict revenge on his enemies. Wisdom is also portrayed as a compensation for the disadvantages of old age. But given the choice, most of us would probably prefer to be younger, rather than gain an understanding of all knowable things.

Wisdom is not a smug cleverness, where we know we were right all along. It's about honestly doing our best to truly understand ourselves and others and how this relates to the world around us.

I suspect we don't need pointy ears or frost-bitten toes to confirm our wisdom. If we made mistakes along the way and learned from them, that's all the qualification we need.

According to the classical Greek philosopher Socrates, a wise person will instinctively lead a simple life. To be successful in the markets we need simple wisdom, not intelligence or cleverness, because successful trading ultimately leads to simplicity regardless of where we begin.

Conclusion

There is no out-of-the-box or off-the-shelf system which will give us an edge in the market. In fact, the secret to successful trading isn't even a secret. All we require is the generosity to open our account, the discipline to follow our strategies, the patience of contentment, the diligence to stay at it, the concentration to do it right and the wisdom to keep it simple. This is the Way of the Trader.

Considering the origin and intended purpose of the Six Paramitas, I was a little hesitant to suggest they be used to help with our trading. Perhaps they will be trampled and clawed by the bulls and bears on Wall Street as we scramble over each other for profits. Besides, there are enough market gurus already without the likes of me plagiarizing the real ones.

On the other hand, there may be more to the Paramitas than meets the eye and they might be more resilient then we think. While we are using them to make some tidy profits in the market, we might also be planting a seed for something greater. After all, they do say, "The lotus flower grows best in the swamp."

SEVEN
RECORDS

A Look at the Records a
Trader Should Keep

S LIPPERY PEOPLE AVOID written records like the plague.
They try to conduct all their business face to face and never
document anything because they know they might have to
deny it later. When traders fail to keep proper records, the only person
they're hoodwinking is themselves.

All traders should keep the following seven records:

1. Trading diary

Personal experience of public events

Have you ever been involved in a large public event and watched the
coverage on TV later that evening? It can feel like you were at a totally
different occurrence because the official version of events doesn't
reflect your personal experience. And therein lies a problem, because
market events for traders are all about personal experience.

Technical and fundamental analysis of the market is the 'TV history' of the past. Bars, lines and moving averages don't capture our experience as the market laid down its track. Three or four long green candles on a chart will never capture the delight we felt as the money flowed into our account. Five red bars, lost among all the others on the far left of the chart, may be the only historical evidence of the week our account was wiped out.

Statistics and charts are far removed from the strong emotions which power the market. These are experienced by us all, but few of us record them. For this reason, we should keep a personal diary when trading. This allows us to create 'our history', which should be read in conjunction with the official statistical version of events.

How much to record in our diary, and when to record it, is a personal decision. The point of the exercise is to capture things which are affecting us now but will not be apparent on the charts later. If we are unsure about recording something, we should err on the side of caution and write it down. Keeping a diary also forces us to think strategically and logically.

Honest records

It's important we are honest with ourselves and record everything. Nobody will see the diary unless we show them, so we have no excuse to hold back. If we are embarrassed by our actions and reluctant to document them, that's a wonderful sign because we know we did something wrong. People who don't get embarrassed never learn from their mistakes.

Good trades and bad trades are not the real issue – the thinking and motivation behind them is what we are trying to identify. Because our diary is recording market events in parallel with our reaction to them, we are examining history from dual perspectives.

When I first started to keep a personal trading diary, it quickly turned into a voluminous file. I meticulously documented everything. I took screenshots of charts, copied and pasted articles, and gave my opinion on every market event. Like a CCTV camera focused on a parking lot, I dutifully recorded everything, even when nothing was happening. Enthusiasm is a healthy sign and we shouldn't beat ourselves up over it. After a while we will learn to record the important stuff and filter out the noise, but we need to maintain our eagerness.

Year-end review

Come December, we should conduct a year-end review of our trading activity. A day or two over the holidays can be set aside for this task. We should get out our trading diary and trade log as we note the high and low points of the year, the mistakes we made, and the lessons learned. From this analysis, we should summarize what we have learned and write these out as bullet points on the last page of the year.

During the following year, we should glance back at these key points (and the points from previous years) to see if we are teaching ourselves anything. And this is the real advantage of a personal trading diary. We are essentially talking to ourselves from the past, trying to learn from our difficult experiences so we won't be destined to repeat them. In fact, the key points from my first few years trading were the foundation for this book.

2. Study notes

When we attend courses or workshops, we should document everything. These days, study material is mostly distributed in soft form because it's convenient for distribution and reduces expenses. But soft copies have one fatal flaw – things which are out of sight tend to be out of mind. I would highly recommend we take the trouble to print our notes and keep them in a folder. A binder with plastic pockets is ideal for this.

During the year, we should periodically flick back over our study notes, especially if we are standing aside waiting for a trading setup to materialize. Glancing through physical paper sheets also offers a welcome break from the screens. We should always be in the process of studying a particular trading topic and we should persevere until we fully understand it.

The more experienced we become, the more we will appreciate and understand the training we received in our early days. Concepts and advice about the market which passed over our head as a beginner will offer fresh insights when we revisit them later.

3. Eight checks

This is a checklist we complete every day before trading. It brings us up to speed with market events and identifies the things we need to know about ourselves and our account before trading. In recognition of their importance, the **Eight Checks** have been given their own chapter and we will be looking at them in greater detail next.

4. Trade log

There are two issues with a trading mistake. The first is making it, the second is not learning from it. Even if the trade is profitable, how can we repeat it if we don't know what we did? An individual record of each trade is known as 'a trade ticket' or 'a trade slip' and are recorded in 'a trade journal' or 'a trade log'. The name is irrelevant so long as we keep a separate record of every trade and store them in a manner which allows detailed analysis.

The important thing is to record why we entered the trade and include a screenshot of the chart and another when we exit. This documents the facts on the chart plus our opinion and interpretation of them.

We can create our own trade log using a spreadsheet which links to image files. Each horizontal line can record a separate trade and the vertical columns should capture all the items mentioned below. However, in order to get the most from our trade records we should be able to analyze them in depth. We need to be able to drill down into the data to calculate success rates on specific risk/reward profiles and strategies.

We do this by sorting and filtering the columns in our spreadsheet, or we can use specific software or an online trade log which performs this function.

At a minimum, each trade ticket should capture the following information:

- **Day, date and time:** Apart from creating chronological records, this will identify if we are trading at specific times rather than waiting for strategic triggers. For example, do we place a trade first thing every Monday morning or at lunchtime on Wednesdays?

- **Account:** We may be trading separate accounts for different markets, currencies or strategies. Some brokers might offer more competitive commissions on some markets or have better access to stocks for shorting.

- **Strategy:** Here, we note which strategy we are trading to identify the most profitable ones. Our account might experience a jump in profits or a drawdown for a period and we need to know if this is related to market conditions or a specific strategy.

- **Market:** Details of the market being traded.

- **Ticker or symbol:** The stock symbol or instrument ticker is enough. After a while many tickers will become familiar as we trade them repeatedly.

- **Direction:** We need to differentiate between long and short trades. For example, we might think we had a balanced year but an analysis could reveal our short trades were twice as profitable as long trades.

- **Source:** Here we record where our trade idea originated. Maybe we have a favorite scan or an indicator triggered an entry. By recording our sources, we can identify the most profitable ones and go back for more.

- **Setup:** This is where we briefly explain why we are making the trade. A detailed description is not required because the setup should relate to the strategy we have already identified above. The setup can be rated based on how many of the required indicators are present. So, the entry here might be as simple as 'No 2 Swing Strategy: 90%.' Comments such as *'I think ABC looks good here'* or *'XYZ is setting up nicely'* is not a valid trading setup!

- **Earnings date:** At this point, we note the next earnings date and place a reminder in our trading calendar. The shorter the time frame we are trading, the more important an earnings announcement is. If the position we are about to open will be held through the next earnings announcement, we need to know exactly how we will deal with that. Now is the time to make the decision rather than waiting for the event to creep up on us.

We have now documented the background to the trade, so next we need to crunch the numbers. Based on our allowable exposure for today, we calculate the size of the position we can open based on our proposed entry price and the location of our protective stop (more about this in the next chapter).

If we are scaling out of positions by taking partial profits, extra columns will be required to calculate the overall profit or loss on the trade. Some online logs incorporate a little widget which calculates all this for us, but the most important thing is to do the calculation.

- **Quantity:** Here, we record the number of shares we traded and the position size.

- **Entry and exit price:** The proposed entry and exit levels, later to be replaced by the actual figures (or both).

- **Entry chart:** An image of our trading chart when we enter and close a trade is invaluable for later examination. Windows 10 has a built-in application for taking a snapshot of a portion of the display on our screen. This can be accessed by clicking the 'Start' button and typing 'Snipping Tool'. On a Mac, pressing SHIFT + CMD + 4 will bring up a crosshairs which we can use to snip a screen image. We should open the captured image of our chart and highlight the indicators which prompted the trade. This image should be saved and linked to the trade ticket.

- **Trade comments:** These are notes which highlight things of interest as we enter the trade. We should also update the notes as the trade progresses. For example, when we move up a stop or take partial profits, we note them here. Finally, we can document why we exited the trade and what order was used.

- **Exit chart:** Again, a snapshot should be taken of the chart when we exit. If we are scaling out, one image when we close out the final portion will do. These images should show sufficient detail that a professional trader will know what your trade plan was just by looking at them.

- **Follow-up date:** Here, we set a date which will remind us to check back on the stock. Depending on the time frame being traded, this might be a few days, weeks or months in the future. This is probably the most important function of our trade records and it benefits us in two separate ways:

(a) After we exit a trade, we need to keep a very close eye on it because it frequently sets up another good entry soon after. When we are looking for something to trade each day, our first port of call should be these closed-out trades. Constantly reviewing our recently closed trades for new opportunities is one of the most profitable things we can do as traders.

Besides, we have already researched and filtered these stocks (more about that later) and set earnings reminders. If they offered good trades yesterday or last week, they are likely to offer more profitable opportunities again soon.

(b) The second benefit of following up on trades happens when we conduct our year-end review. Knowing we made or lost money is not enough – we need to know exactly where it was made and lost. When we sort our closed trades by strategy, direction and profitability, some very interesting insights can be gained. However, when creating our trade tickets, we should remember the data junkie's dictum, 'Garbage in, garbage out.' We need to keep the information concise and relevant so as to facilitate easy analysis later.

Trades should be analyzed in blocks of ten or 20, rather than looking at each trade in isolation. In this way, the outcome of one individual trade (and our emotional relationship with it) is almost irrelevant, as the emphasis is on the discipline of following our strategy.

5. Our equity curve

All traders should create a spreadsheet and record the closing balance of their account every month. These figures should be plotted on a graph. This is an **equity curve** and it's what trading is all about. If our equity is not rising, we are wasting our time.

As the months progress, the curve should be climbing to the right. At worst, it should be flat. If it is falling to the right, we need to stop trading. If we are unable or unwilling to create this graph, we most likely have a gambling issue and should avoid the financial markets.

If a trader blows out his account and starts again when his finances improve, he should continue his equity curve from the point where his previous account ended by adjusting the new balance to reflect the cash deposit.

The spreadsheet should have the date in the first column and the closing account balance in the next column. Then we should plot a graph with the date on the horizontal axis and the account balance on the vertical axis. When we lodge or withdraw funds, the balance should be adjusted accordingly, so an additional column for the 'adjusted balance' should be added. If we are holding an account balance in different currencies, we can filter out the impact of currency movements with the addition of another column for our 'base currency balance'.

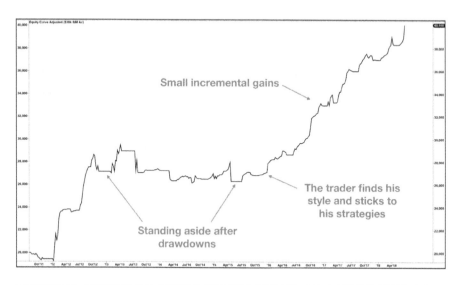

FIGURE 14: SMOOTHLY RISING EQUITY CURVE ON A SIMULATED $20K ACCOUNT

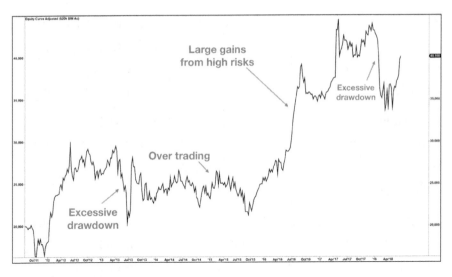

FIGURE 15: JAGGED EQUITY CURVE ON THE SAME ACCOUNT

Apart from the direction of our equity curve, we also need to be aware of its shape. When trading other people's capital, a smooth and rising equity curve is the most sought-after qualification. Jagged equity curves with sudden jumps in profit and sharp drawdowns make investors nervous. Admittedly, the overall trend of a spiky curve might be up, but people like things to run smoothly, especially when their money is on the line – literally.

In the equity curves shown above, both traders are equally profitable but the top curve (figure 14) offers a better night's sleep because the trader takes smaller risks and stays in cash more often.

A smoothly rising equity curve can be created by maintaining a constant risk size on each trade and by scaling out of profitable positions. When we trade a full position size and let it run until the trade is closed, our equity curve will take a sudden jump. We also run the risk of having the trade go against us and losing all the profits. If we take partial profits as the trade progresses, not only are we taking some risk off the table, but the incremental gains will smoothen our equity curve and calm the nerves of our financial backers.

If we have placed funds with a money manager, we should create an equity curve using their monthly statements to gauge their performance. Based on the profile of the investment, we can add the appropriate index or benchmark to the graph. Not only will this keep track of how the investment is going, but it will give us something interesting to discuss when we meet them next.

6. Trading strategies

When we trade, our mission is not to make money, it's to **follow the strategy**. Our mission statement is when we write down that strategy in such a way, we could hand it to another trader and they could use it immediately without any further explanation. A documented strategy clearly lays out what we are doing, why we are doing it and when we should be doing it.

The written strategy should contain at least the following key elements:

Name and revision

Every strategy should have a name which resonates with us on a personal level, so we can take ownership of it. This might be something like 'Daily Swing Strategy No 1' or 'Trend Following Strategy A'. Personally, I like to use a name which captures the philosophy behind the strategy and summarizes what it's supposed to be doing.

We should also have a method for revision control which tracks any adjustments we made to the strategy since its inception. I find the numbering sequence used for software releases – where the first digit donates a major change and the second records minor adjustments – works very well (e.g. Tidal Strategy 1.3). Revision control also serves as a reminder we are not supposed to be tampering with our strategies in the first place.

General trading rules

These are universal to all strategies, so it's no harm to have them in clear view at the top of the document to serve as a reminder. Our general trading rules might be something like this:

- round positions to nearest multiple of 50

- do not move stop closer to price

- don't trade on Monday morning

- maintain constant position size

- only trade filtered stocks

- follow the five limits of risk.

Source/scan

Under this heading we clearly explain how we find trades for the strategy. It might be a special scan or another reliable source which has proven profitable in the past.

Indicators

In this section, we list the technical indicators required to trade this strategy and the settings required for each.

Entry and exit criteria

Here we state exactly what needs to happen for us to enter a trade, what to look for as the trade plays out, and what signs will confirm we need to exit the trade.

Comments

Finally, our documented strategy can record some observations and insights we have gained from trading the strategy in the past. This might be something like, 'This strategy works best after a market correction' or maybe, 'Do not use this strategy when 75% of stocks are trading above their 50-day moving average.'

7. *Manually sourced data*

We touched on this already in the **Five Stages** chapter when we discussed end-of-day data. I refer to this as 'manually sourced' because we make the effort to go and gather it, rather than having our trading platform give it to us. This data can be anything from EOD data about markets or individual stocks, to economic statistics or company fundamentals.

These records build up slowly over time, so they should be stored in a format which will allow easy analysis or charting. We might be the only one collecting this data, so it's good practice to keep three copies: one on our computer hard drive which is synced to a copy in the cloud and another on an external hard drive or third-party backup facility. As another layer of safety, we should email copies of the most important documents to ourselves weekly.

EIGHT CHECKS

A Comprehensive Pre-Trading Checklist

W E SHOULD NEVER trade unless we analyze ourselves and the market beforehand. This is especially important if we have been out of touch for a while. A pre-trading checklist is the best way to prepare for the trading day ahead. Not only will this bring us up to speed, it will also put us in the correct frame of mind.

Our analysis needs to be comprehensive enough to capture everything of importance, while being compact enough to get through relatively quickly. The more streamlined it is, the more likely we are to use it.

Each of us needs to develop our own checklist based on the markets we trade and our personality. At a bare minimum, the checklist should examine ourselves, the market and our current financial position. If we normally trade a single currency pair or just one instrument, the checklist will be short. If we are trading multiple markets, the checklist will be pretty heavy and we will be reluctant to go through it every day, that in itself should raise a warning flag.

Background

In March 2014, Dr. Alexander Elder shared his checklist at a workshop in the Netherlands. His background as a medical doctor and practicing psychiatrist is reflected in the structured and systematic approach he takes to trading. I found his method of self-analysis especially useful. We trade similar markets, so with Dr. Elder's kind permission I adopted his format and used it as a foundation for my checklist.

The **Eight Checks** are on a spreadsheet with a fixed vertical column on the left – we complete the next column to the right every day we trade. As the days progress, we insert a new column each time and a record of our analysis is pushed out to the right. In this way, we get a handle on what's going on today, but we can also view the rolling progress of the results at a glance.

More importantly, as we generate this checklist we are also laying out a history where our personal analysis is recorded in parallel with the market. This proves especially useful when there is a sudden market move. We can look back to our analysis to see if anything we examined beforehand gave an indication of the unfolding event. If it did, we know what to keep doing. If it didn't, we need to start looking at other sources of information.

As the trading days go by and the spreadsheet starts to develop a back story, we can identify trends which may not be apparent when recording one figure at a time. If our charting platform allows the importing of third-party data, we can import data from our checklist and overlay it on our trading charts. In this way, we can start to create our own technical indicators which nobody else will be using.

Over time the checklist will evolve based on our experience and the markets we are trading. The checklist detailed below is for U.S. equities and there are 37 items I look at each morning. That may sound like a lot, but we can get through it very quickly. Each item is a separate row on the spreadsheet, but they are grouped into sections. The number of items we examine will change depending on the market, but the eight sections remain constant – hence the **Eight Checks** title.

DAY / DATE	Friday 19 Oct 2018	Thursday 18 Oct 2018	Wednesday 17 Oct 2018	Tuesday 16 Oct 2018	Monday 15 Oct 2018	Friday 12 Oct 2018	Thursday 11 Oct 2018	Wednesday 10 Oct 2018	Tuesday 09 Oct 2018	Monday 08 Oct
1. MYSELF	Myself	Myself	Myself	Myself	Myself	Myself	Myself	Myself	Myself	
Mindfulness	15 mins	11 mins	15 mins	8 mins	10 mins		6 mins	5 mins	12 mins	1(
Experience	Busy day, backtesting	Busy, no new positions	Traded bounce	Anticipating bounce	Alert, relaxed		Busy, travel	Very Profitable	Have patience	Bus
2. MACRO	Macro	Macro	Macro	Macro	Macro	Macro	Macro	Macro	Macro	
Econ Calendar 1	Existing home sales	Jobs	FOMC, Housing Starts	Ind Production	Retail Sales 08:30		CPI,Jobs, EIA	PPI, FD	No	US Bo
Econ Calendar 2	CN GDP	Ditto	EIA Report	Earnings & IP	Earnings & RS		Ditto	Ditto	No	
3. MARKET	Macro	Macro	Macro	Market	Market	Market	Market	Market	Market	M
Asia Pacific	Mixed -0.56/2.98%	Down -0.80/-2.94%	Up 0.06/1.29%	Mixed -0.86/1.25%	Down -1.49/-1.87		Down -5.2%/-3.89	Up 0.21/0.16%	Up 0.15/0.18%	Tokyo Clos
Europe	Up 0.15/0.56%	Down -0.12/-0.23%	Down -0.10%	Mixed -0.16/0.30%	Up 0.17 to 0.40%		Down -1.47/-1.94%	Down 1.27/-2.21%	Up 0.05/0.25%	Down -1
Gold	1230.80	1226.10	1230.20	1290.60	1223.70		1197.50	1193.60	1193.40	12
Oil Futures (WTI)	69.20	68.97	71.58	71.88	72.24		72.68	74.75	74.28	1
Euro/Dollar	1.147	1.149	1.156	1.159	1.160		1.151	1.149	1.152	1
10 Yr US Treasury Notes	118'01.5	117'28.5	118'03.5	118'03.0	118'08.5		117'24.0	117'26.0	117'22.5	11
10 Yr US Treasury Note Yield	31.75	31.98	31.56	31.63	31.41		32.25	32.08	32.25	C
S&P500 & ATR Position	2769 -2ATR	2809 -1ATR	2810 -1ATR	2751 -3ATR	2767 -3ATR		2785 -3.5ATR	2880 -1ATR	2884 -1ATR	288
NASDAQ & ATR Position	7485 -2ATR	7642 -1ATR	7645 -1ATR	7431 -3ATR	7497 -2.5ATR		7422 -4ATR	7738 -2ATR	7736 -2ATR	778
Russell 2000 & ATR Position	1561 -3ATR	1589 -1.5ATR	1597 -1.5ATR	1553 -4ATR	1546 -5ATR		1575 -4.5ATR	1621 -3ATR	1629 -3ATR	163
% US Issues Above 50DEMA	17.86	23.61	21.61	16.56	15.81		18.35	26.81	28.13	
Composite Help (Weekly Sum)	-50.97	-71.85	-88.80	-92.89	-96.11		-64.76	-48.42	-49.76	
Composite Help	-10.48	-4.04	-3.99	-9.86	-22.59		-20.99	-8.08	-13.08	
Volatility (VIX)	19.43	18.02	17.85	20.40	21.97		22.96	15.95	15.69	
US Futures (Average)	Up 0.49%	Down -0.37%	Down -0.46%	Up 0.35%	Down -0.34%		Down -0.81%	Down 1.89%	Flat	Up
4. METHODS	Methods	Methods	Methods	Methods	Methods	Methods	Methods	Methods	Methods	M
Tidal Strategy	ON	ON	ON	ON	ON		ON	ON	ON	
Help-Up Strategy	ON	ON	ON	OFF	OFF		OFF	OFF	OFF	
Help-Down Strategy	OFF	OFF	OFF	OFF	OFF		ON	ON	ON	
5. MONEY	Money	Money	Money	Money	Money	Money	Money	Money	Money	M
Month Opening Account Balance	50,000	50,000	50,000	50,000	50,000		50,000	50,000	50,000	5(
Current Account Balance	51,102	51,882	52,003	51,984	52,081		52,131	51,783	51,226	5(
Monthly Gain (Loss) %	2.20	3.76	4.01	3.97	4.16		4.26	3.57	2.45	
Current Exposure	672	1,089	1,352	602	602		689	728	787	
Available Exposure	2,328	1,911	1,648	2,398	2,398		2,311	2,272	2,213	2
Risk per Trade (1.5%)	767	778	780	780	781		782	777	768	
Cash Balance	28,651	28,651	28,651	36,305	38,305		18,023	18,023	18,023	1
Margin Balance	102,204	103,764	104,006	103,968	104,162		104,262	103,566	102,452	10
6. MEMOS	Memos	Memos	Memos	Memos	Memos	Memos	Memos	Memos	Memos	M
Earnings Alerts	AAPL, JNJ, ADP, AET	AAPL, JNJ, ADP, AET	AAPL, JNJ, ADP, AET	AAPL, JNJ, ADP, AET	AAPL, JNJ, ADP, AET		AAPL, JNJ, ADP, AET	AAPL, JNJ, ADP, AET	AAPL, JNJ, ADP, AET	AAPL, JN
All Orders Active	Yes	Yes	Yes	Yes	Yes		Yes	Yes	Yes	M
7. MENTORS & MATES	Mentors	Mentors	Mentors	Mentors	Mentors	Mentors	Mentors	Mentors	Mentors	M

FIGURE 16: EXAMPLE OF AN EIGHT CHECKS SPREADSHEET FOR A $50,000 ACCOUNT TRADING US EQUITIES

Day and date

Having said that, the first two rows on the list are not in any section, because this is where we enter today's day and date. We type out the **day** in full to remind ourselves that Mondays and Fridays are important. Everyone piles in on Monday as the flood gates open, but accounts (and scores) are settled on Friday. We might also want to develop an indicator which records how the market performed on different days of the week, so a separate entry for 'day' will be useful in the future.

Recording the **date** will remind us if we are nearing month end or if a public holiday or earnings season is pending. If we are trading overseas markets, daylight saving time also needs to be considered. For example, Europe currently makes the switch on the last Sunday in March and the last Sunday in October, whereas the U.S. switches on the second Sunday in March and the first Sunday in November.[1] We should set reminders in our trading calendar for these switchover dates.

1. Myself

The first order of business is to turn our attention inward, so I do a **mindfulness** practice for about five minutes. We also need to create a break between what we were doing previously and the activity of trading.

Not only is mindfulness a practice of concentration, it is also a state of awareness. So next, we examine our **experience** – Dr. Elder suggests we consider things like our physical condition, our previous day's trading, our overall mood and our schedule for the day ahead. At this

---

[1] Daylight saving time is observed in many countries but a number are currently reviewing the issue. Russia and Belarus ended the practice in 2014 and the EU has plans to end it in 2019.

point we should also pay special attention to our level of anxiety about open positions and reduce our capital at risk if we are uncomfortable.

2. *Macro*

Next, we examine the economic calendar for any upcoming market-moving events. This section comes first because a major event like a highly-anticipated interest rate announcement or an important OPEC meeting may prompt us not to trade today.

Many websites offer good **macroeconomic calendars** for free, but we need to ensure the information is accurate and everything is covered for the market we are trading. For this reason, I always check two separate websites. The impact of events are usually rated by the information provider and the same events can be rated differently. This serves as a reminder that nobody knows for sure how the market will respond to an event.

Scheduled events should never catch us unawares. We are never surprised to discover today is our birthday, likewise we should never be caught off guard by the market calendar. We have no excuse because market-moving events happen on a regular basis and can leave havoc in their wake. This occurs because stop-loss orders which have lain dormant and cozy under support zones for months are suddenly exposed to the glaring sunlight of the market when a macro event lifts the lid on everything.

Trading firms use innovative techniques to get their staff in tune with the market calendar. Some companies have friendly competitions around macroeconomic events, where everyone guesses the pending figure and explains why they chose that number. The winner then gets a token prize and some bragging rights at the water cooler. This is also a useful method for a firm to gauge the level of consensus among their traders.

If we are trading overseas markets, unfamiliar public holidays are something else to bear in mind. At the beginning of each new trading year, we should look up the pending public holidays for the foreign markets we trade and set reminders for the next 12 months.

3. Market

The trading day doesn't just start from a standing stop, like a sprinter out of the blocks. Sentiment passes from one financial center to the next, like relay runners handing over the baton. When we step up to our trading desk, we are stepping into the middle of an evolving, highly competitive and complex environment. For this, we need to be prepared.

In this section, we examine economic and technical indicators relevant to the market and instruments we will be trading. Obviously, the checks will vary depending on our preferred market, but we need to be sure we capture everything at this point. This will include market indices and trends, some market internals and a few individual indicators we trust.

For example, when trading U.S. markets, we might begin with other **international indices, currency pairs, precious metals, oil, U.S. 10-year bonds, interest rates** and **volatility**. Then we should check specific monthly, weekly and daily levels on **S&P 500 (SPX), Nasdaq (IXIC)** and **Russell 2000 (RUT)** indices.

Next, we might check economic sectors and I use SPDR ETFs for this, so I can see everything at a glance and note how each is performing relative to the others. I also note the location of major and minor support and resistance levels, and check the futures for each index mentioned above, to see how the market is likely to open. Finally, I refer to my HELP indicators and other market internal indicators which we will examine in greater detail in **The Strategies** chapter.

4. *Methods*

Having examined the market, we need to decide what we're going to do about it (if anything). In this section, our favorite strategies are listed and we confirm if each is in a 'risk-on' or 'risk-off' mode. This means we can or can't trade it today, or if we already have a position open. We then assign a color to each row accordingly. Green means we can trade that strategy today, orange means not today but maybe soon, and red means no trading. If we are looking at a block of red or orange, today is a day for paperwork, a day for analysis and research – it's not a day for trading.

If we plotted this sequence of colors under a market index, it should concur with the oscillations and trends in the market. If a pattern is not obvious, then our methods are wrong.

5. *Money*

This is the point where our risk management rules get serious, because they now apply to the cash in our account. This section of the checklist has eight rows and the first records our **month opening a/c balance.** This is the balance in our account on the final day of the previous month and will be our baseline figure for the current month. We should lock the contents of this cell.

In the cell below that, we enter our **current a/c balance.** This includes the current value of all open positions and our cash balance. If we are trading shares, the values will be fixed before the market opens. If we are trading futures or forex it will be a moving target, so we have to pick a value we feel is appropriate.

In the third cell – **monthly gain/loss %** – we should have a formula embedded which calculates how much we are up or down in percentage terms since the beginning of the month. At a glance, we can see if we are approaching the 6% cut-off point for monthly losses.

Next, we check our **current exposure** to the market, in cash terms. Exposure is the difference in cash between the current price of a position we hold and the protective stop, multiplied by the number of shares. We add this up for all the positions we currently have open. If all our protective stops are hit today, this figure is the minimum amount we will be down.

Under that we have available exposure, where we calculate how much additional risk we can take on today – if any. Our entire exposure in the market at any given time should never be such that we could lose more than 6% of our month opening account balance.

In the next cell, we calculate what our trade risk should be in cash terms for each new position we are about to open today. This should be no more than 2% of our current a/c balance. We use our current balance rather than the opening balance because ongoing losses and gains are factored in.

The next cell shows the cash balance in our account and this will confirm if we have funds available to open new positions or if recently closed trades have been settled. Finally, we note our margin balance, which indicates how much our broker is prepared to loan us.

6. Memos

There are two rows in this section.

(a) The first is to confirm **earnings** reminders are set for all our open positions. When we have been using our **Eight Checks** for a while, all the alerts start triggering around the same time of year and this helps to get our mind in sync with earnings season.

(b) Next, we confirm our **open orders** are still live and have been received by our broker before the market opens. On occasion, our trading platform can crash and orders get 'lost'. A frequent mistake is to set up a protective stop as a 'day' order which expires at the close when we intended to use a 'good till canceled' (GTC) order which stays open until activated or canceled.

7. Mentors and mates

Sometimes, we check-in with other traders whose opinions we value. Each trading style has a specific way of looking at the market and by consulting professionals who trade the same style as us we can get a fresh perspective. We may agree or disagree with their analysis, but that's not the point: it's about identifying opportunities which we may have overlooked.

When we hear about the recent trading experience of others, we also have access to an informal market internal indicator. When the market is going higher, but good traders are not finding good trades, this is a sure sign something is amiss under the surface.

Money managers email monthly newsletters to their clients which usually contain a market opinion based on fundamental analysis. At this point on the checklist, I bring to mind the current opinion of one or two managers whose analysis I respect and consider this in the context of what I'm hearing from traders.

8. Media

We should try not to get caught up in day-to-day financial news stories. As we saw earlier, it's the market's reaction to the news that matters, rather than the news itself. However, in the final section of the checklist, there's no harm in consulting the crisis crew. There are two reasons we do this:

(a) It's quite possible the macroeconomic calendars we reviewed earlier have missed something completely or have underestimated the importance of an event.

(b) We get a feel for how important the trading public are likely to rate the event. When something is getting blanket coverage by the financial media and dominates the headlines, the market reaction is likely to be exaggerated.

Conclusion

This checklist might sound like a lot of work, especially when we are keen to start trading and we haven't kept a checklist in the past. But you can do the checks in under ten minutes (excluding the mindfulness practice), and setting aside time to find the answers is just as important as the answers themselves. It forces us to draw a line under what we were doing previously.

The important thing is to complete the list in full and not get drawn off on tangents (especially when looking at websites). It establishes a pattern where we begin to understand the market without having to rely on others.

In Chinese culture, the number eight is considered very lucky because the Mandarin word for eight (*bā*), has a similar sound to the word *fā* which means 'wealth' or 'prosper'. The **Eight Checks** have kept me out of harm's way and brought prosperity to my trading on more than one occasion.

NINE FILTERS

Selecting Which Stocks to Trade Using Filters

CCORDING TO MEMBERS of the World Federation of Exchanges, there were 51,923 companies listed on 82 global exchanges in November 2018.[1] We need stocks which offer profitable trading opportunities, but we can't trade them all – the solution is a filter.

Filtering stocks is a process where we start out with everything available and reduce it to a list we can work with. It's not a case of deciding which market to trade, it's more a case of finding stocks and exchanges which offer the liquidity and stability we require.

Filters remove unwanted and uncooperative stocks. In the process they also reduce the choice on offer. This is a good thing, as too many options frequently lead to bad decisions. Ideally, we should have about 100 stocks for each strategy we trade, and have our scanners set to cycle through them repeatedly looking for opportunities.

---

[1]   World Federation of Exchanges, November 2018 (www.world-exchanges.org/home/index.php/statistics/monthly-reports).

In this way, rather than going into the market everyday looking for something to trade, we are presented with a list of candidates which exhibit the traits we require. On the days we are shown a very short list (or no list at all), it means the current market is not conducive to the strategy.

The concept of filtering stocks and then only working from the pre-selected basket was shown to me by Kerry Lovvorn, at his office in Alabama. Like all great ideas, it's obvious when someone shows it to us, but we would never think of it ourselves.

Character reference

Each stock has its own personality and we need to examine them closely before we undertake a journey together. A stock might look good on the surface, but it may not possess the depth of character to weather the storms we will encounter in the market. For example, highly volatile stocks are good for day trading as we need sudden sharp moves to make a profit.

However, it will be difficult to get on with a mercurial stock for an extended period of time, so low-volatility stocks which tend to trend are more suited to long-term relationships.

The characteristics we are looking for change according to the strategy, but the filtering process remains the same. We should maintain a separate list of stocks (watchlist) for each strategy we trade and run a strategy-specific filter each quarter.

When a stock is brought to our attention and it's not on our watchlist, we should run it through our filter. If it comes out the other side, only then should we consider it. After a while we know exactly what we're looking for, so a quick glance will rule it in or out.

The filtering process

There are numerous free and subscription-based online resources which allow us to filter stocks. Many trading platforms also offer screening applications as part of their overall package. It's unlikely one single resource will perform all the steps we require. It's a case of creating our own process by using elements from various sources.

The filter process has nine stages which are divided into two steps. The first is a general filter which applies to all stocks, the second uses specific filters to fine-tune watchlists for strategies. The filter should be carried out four times a year after earnings season.

Earnings and guidance

Share prices are based on expectations of future earnings. When firms announce earnings for the previous quarter, many also provide guidance for the next one. Earnings are a factual statement of the financial performance of a firm for the past three months, whereas guidance is an indication of what the company believes will happen in the next quarter.

In theory, following an earnings announcement, the market instantly adjusts the previous expectation to the current reality and the whole process of new expectations begins again.

However, earnings are based on a past which is no longer relevant (because we can't trade in the past) and guidance is an insider's educated guess on the future (a form of financial science fiction). For this reason, the share price of any given stock is always detached from reality and frantically seeking its true value.

Earnings season

Firms can release earnings at any time and the numbers are always trickling in, but the major announcements come in from the middle of January, April, July and October onwards. Therefore, I run the filter at the latter end of February, May, August and November – secure in the knowledge that market prices reflect recent earnings.

Step one: general filter

1. Ethics and eccentrics

There are some who hold the view that the financial markets are the ugly face of capitalism. I don't agree. The markets are like crooked teeth: they're not pretty but they're real and they work. The markets are millions of traders and investors, regular folk trying to make their way in the world like the rest of us. Granted, there are a few wolves and vultures in the mix (not to mention a few robots), but I am unaware of any profession where only saints are welcome.

For good or for bad, the markets are here to stay, and they are growing bigger and more influential. We have to deal with them as best we can and take responsibility for our trading. Accordingly, we can exclude specific activities or individual firms which are in conflict with our conscience.

These may be firms involved in defense, alcohol, tobacco, gambling or adult entertainment. It might be a particular chemical or pharmaceutical firm, or some other company we don't like. I even know people who don't trade soft commodity futures such as corn, wheat and soybeans because of their impact on food prices.

Stocks are grouped into economic sectors such as basic materials, conglomerates, consumer goods, financial, healthcare, industrial goods, services, technology and utilities. They are further classified into 150–200 business-specific industry groups (depending on the classification standard being used),[2] so we can remove an entire industry group if needs be.

With a clear conscience, we can then proceed to the next step, which is to exclude the stocks which are highly unpredictable. These can be stocks which are always in the news and their valuations are based on questionable future earnings and elevated expectations. Perhaps they are at the cutting edge of a new technological breakthrough or they are going to 'disrupt' an industry. As these stocks climb higher, the more pronounced the disappointment will be when it eventually arrives.

Biotechnology is an area which merits a cautious approach. Not to be confused with established pharmaceutical firms, 'biotechs' are in the business of developing new drugs and conducting clinical research. When everything hinges around a single drug trial, we are taking a big risk by trading these shares. Traders who specialize in this area know the individual firms and their research well, and use specific strategies to trade them.

In terms of risk, smaller exploration and mining stocks can be similar to biotechs in that everything can hinge on the result of one test. If a speculative drilling rig strikes out or a soil sample from a new mine contains nothing but soil, these stocks lose their shine instantly.

2. Exchange-traded funds (ETFs)

ETFs are listed on stock exchanges and trade like a share, so they will automatically be included in the filtering process. Because they track a basket of assets, we need to fully understand each one if it's

---

2 There are three main industry classification standards. In the financial markets, the Global Industry Classification Standard (GICS) developed in 1999 by MSCI and Standard & Poor's (S&P) and the Industry Classification Benchmark (ICB) maintained by FTSE Russell are commonly used. The Standard Industrial Classification (SIC) tends to be used more by government agencies. Each classification is constantly under review and updated to reflect industry developments.

going to make it to our watchlist. Remember, trading is all about risk management and if we don't know what the risk is, we can't manage it.

One way to deal with this is to separate ETFs from stocks at the outset by creating a special watchlist, as they often require a strategy which is specific to each one. ETFs are great for gaining access to commodities and indices if we feel we are not ready to trade futures.

3. Size

Market capitalization and **shareholder equity** are two measures which allow us to calculate the size of a company. Capitalization is obtained by multiplying today's share price by the number of shares outstanding. Shareholder equity is a more accurate measure and is simply the company assets less the liabilities. However, capitalization can be calculated quickly and constantly so it features prominently on screening programs.

Capitalization falls into six broad groups (depending on who's doing the grouping) and can be roughly broken down as follows:

- mega: greater than $200bn

- large: $10bn–$200bn

- mid: $2bn–$10bn

- small: $300m–$2bn

- micro: $50m–$300m

- nano: less than $50m.

Market cap changes on an hourly basis and during market pullbacks the media love to report, '*Billions Wiped off Value of Shares.*' That's never true. Billions were wiped off the *price*; the underlying 'value' of the firms remained more or less the same. In the next chapter, we will explore how the difference between price and value applies to trading.

Rather than getting caught up with market cap, we should just filter for a specific level. Personally, I avoid firms below $300m. Obviously, we can trade smaller firms, but the risk increases as the market cap reduces. A rising tide lifts all boats, but a storm sinks the small ones first.

4. Liquidity

In the **five limits of risk** we discussed the importance of liquidity and how we need orders to be filled quickly and accurately. However, liquidity isn't only about price and volume. The instruments we trade must also have 'depth', which means there are an abundance of orders stacked above and below the current price.

'Resiliency,' which is an instrument's ability to absorb a huge order and keep going as before, is also important. The difference (**spread**) between the price traders are willing to sell at (**ask**) and the price other traders are willing to pay (**bid**) must also be very close.

The classic (if rather tasteless) example used to demonstrate the importance of liquidity, is a fire in a movie theatre. Nobody wants out until everybody wants out. When someone shouts 'fire' and the exit door is small, many of the moviegoers will get badly burned.

Let's say we want to open a $5,000 position in a stock which is trading at $2 with an average volume of 60,000 shares per day. Our order will be for 2,500 shares which represents more than 4% of average daily volume. Let's now assume we place the order during lunchtime, when volumes on the exchange are light. Until our order is filled, we are the entire market for that stock at that point in time.

This is all very well when we are buying in a quiet market. But what happens a few weeks later when fire breaks out and our protective stop loss order is triggered? An order is automatically sent to the exchange with instructions to sell at the current price, which is dropping. If we are running for the exit, we will not be alone. With all those sell orders hitting the exchange at once, buyers will not be plentiful or generous. Ouch!

Another reason to avoid illiquid stocks is their tendency to negate the validity of technical indicators. Technical analysis is essentially the historical price of an asset presented in visual form. Indicators are overlaid on the price data in an attempt to identify recurring patterns. However, just like statistics, technical analysis is only reliable and actionable when drawn from a large data set. Very few trades produce very little data.

PENNY STOCKS[3]

Low-priced and low-volume stocks tend to 'gap' a lot. A gap occurs when the share price takes a large jump from one price to another without trading anywhere in between. This often happens when news is released overnight, and the market opens in the morning at a very different price. This can play havoc with our account as the price jumps over our orders.

In addition, penny stocks, like cheap liquor stores, tend to attract unsavory types. Prices are easily manipulated by unscrupulous insiders and opportunistic outsiders. 'Pump n' dump' scams on low-priced, thinly-traded stocks are easy to execute. These days, social media platforms are awash with this type of activity targeting inexperienced millennial traders.

---

3   US Securities and Exchange Commission (SEC): "The term 'penny stock' generally refers to a security issued by a very small company that trades at less than $5 per share." (www.sec.gov/fast-answers/answerspennyhtm.html)
New York Stock Exchange (NYSE) Rule 7.6: "The minimum price variation ('MPV') for quoting and entry of orders in securities traded on the Exchange is $0.01, with the exception of securities that are priced less than $1.00 for which the MPV for quoting and entry of orders is $0.0001."
NASDAQ Stock Exchange Rule 4701(k): "The term 'minimum price increment' means $0.01 in the case of a System Security priced at $1 or more per share, and $0.0001 in the case of a System Security priced at less than $1 per share."

Another issue with low-priced stocks is the way they move on the exchange. High-priced, high-volume stocks flow strongly and smoothly, like a freight train on a track. Their poorer cousins don't flow, they stumble and jump like pack mules on a mountain trail.

On a $2 stock, a move of a few cents can have a profound effect in percentage terms. There are only 40 five-cent increments and each five-cent move is a 2.5% change in price. As the price gets lower, each five-cent move becomes an even larger percentage. U.S. stock exchanges will fill an order to the nearest $0.01 for stocks over $1 and $0.0001 below that, but the orders for low-priced stocks tend to be clustered at round numbers. So, when the price moves up or down, it doesn't flow smoothly – it jumps from one cluster of orders to another.

BLUE-CHIP STOCKS[4]

Blue-chip stocks are a totally different ball game because they attract institutional investors who take a long-term view and do their homework before committing to anything. Institutions and funds make their decisions by committee, which applies a sort of inertia to the shares they hold. When a fire breaks out, they don't stampede for the exit – they calmly assess the situation as they stroll to the fire extinguisher. This provides nimble traders plenty of time to get out.

---

4   NASDAQ, definition of a blue-chip stock: "Common stock of well-known companies with a history of growth and dividend payments." (www.investopedia. com/terms/b/bluechipstock.asp)

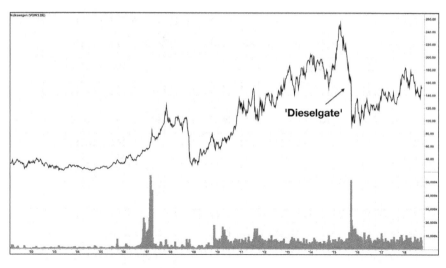

FIGURE 17: CHART OF VOLKSWAGEN (XETRA: VOW3) 2001–2018

A case in point is Volkswagen (VOW3.DE). Over the weekend of 19 and 20 September 2015, the Environmental Protection Agency (EPA) in the U.S. called a halt to emissions rigging by software in diesel engines manufactured by VW. When the Frankfurt market opened on Monday 21 September, VW shares gapped down over 13% and by Wednesday 23 September they were down over 40%. Considering the size, reputation and influence of this company, a drop of that magnitude was enormous. But not all price drops are created equal.

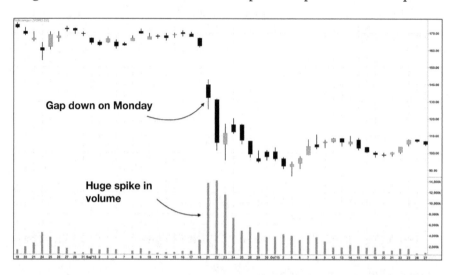

FIGURE 18: DAILY CHART OF VW DURING 'DIESELGATE'

After the initial gap down on Monday morning, the price recovered a little and continued downwards for three days, but at a more controlled pace. Over 13m shares traded hands on Monday, 14m on Tuesday and 11m on Wednesday – as opposed to an average of 3m per day before the news broke. After the gap down, and in spite of the huge volume of trading, the price slowly keeled over like a tree falling, rather than continuing to drop like a stone.

Over the course of the three days, some shareholders rushed for the door, some strolled and some stayed put. Because of the high liquidity in the stock and the ability of the exchange to process the transactions, those who ran for the door found it was very large. A trader holding a long position in VW, using proper risk management, would have taken only a 3–4% drawdown on their account even if their order was filled at the worst price on Monday.

THE FIRST LIMIT OF RISK

As mentioned in the five limits of risk, our position must be less than 1% of the daily turnover in a stock, known in the U.S. as 'dollar value traded'.

The 1% liquidity rule will also ensure we only trade on the largest exchanges. Small domestic stock markets are more suited to long-term investing and traders prefer the liquidity and regulation of larger international stock exchanges.

In order of size by domestic market capitalization in U.S. dollars, the largest exchanges are NYSE, Nasdaq U.S., Japan Exchange Group, Shanghai Stock Exchange, Euronext, LSE Group, Hong Kong Exchanges and Clearing, Shenzhen Stock Exchange, TMX Group, BSE India, National Stock Exchange of India and Deutsche Boerse.[5]

---

5   World Federation of Exchanges, 2018.

Low-priced stocks can have a sudden spike in price or volume, so they might technically pass the 1% liquidity test. Bear in mind when we refer to the 'volume' of a stock, we are usually referring to the average daily volume for the past three months. A spike in activity for a few days can significantly affect the calculation and make the stock look more liquid than it actually is.

We shouldn't just look at the current price and volume without putting them in context.

In terms of liquidity, we can think of price as the height of our exit door and volume as the width. As the price and volume of a stock start dropping, the door starts shrinking. We must never allow ourselves to be in a position where our trade is too tall or too fat for the door.

5. Profitability

We can filter for profitability in different ways, such as earnings per share growth, return on assets, return on equity, return on investment, gross margin or sales growth. We are looking for companies who actually make a profit or break even at worst. We know share prices are based on expected future earnings, so if a company has current earnings, they most likely have a future.

The dotcom bubble of 1997–2001 was partly caused by market expectation that unprofitable internet companies would eventually take over the world and make huge profits along the way. The takeover is going according to plan, but the profits were elusive back then.

If a firm is not making a profit, as short-term shareholders we need to ask what is the point of it? Where is the premium we expect to be paid for holding the risk? We are not key suppliers or insiders who will still be paid even when the firm is losing money. Remember, we will be running this filter every three months, so a good stock which goes through a bad patch will eventually get back on our watchlist when profitability returns.

A quick and simple method is to scan for **operating margin**[6] – we should filter for a margin which is at least positive. This will give us an indication of how much a firm makes (before interest and taxes) on each dollar of sales. We like to believe the majority of firms are profitable, but when we look at the 5,082 listings on the AMEX, NASDAQ and NYSE exchanges in the U.S. (excluding ETFs), just 3,025 have a positive operating margin. On that basis, our profitability scan would exclude over 40% of all U.S. listings in one fell swoop.[7]

6. Liquidity ratios

Not to be confused with the liquidity of a firm's shares, liquidity ratios measure a company's ability to pay its debts and its margin of safety. Depending on the level of detail offered by our scanning software, we can look at **current ratio** which assesses a company's ability to meet its short-term obligations by dividing its current assets by its current liabilities.

We might also scan for **quick ratio**. This looks at the most liquid assets by deducting a firm's inventories from the assets before looking at the liabilities. The higher the quick ratio, the stronger the company position. In both cases, we should be looking for a ratio over one.

Step two: strategy-specific filters

At this stage, we should have reduced the original list significantly. In some cases, there might be nothing left. The capitalization, price and volume levels we choose will often exclude entire markets, especially the smaller exchanges. If this is the case, rather than adjusting our filter settings, we need to seriously reconsider the market we are trading.

---

6   Operating margin (www.investopedia.com/terms/o/operatingmargin.asp).

7   Finviz.com, Scanner, 14 September 2018.

From this point on, we will be using filters which relate specifically to strategies. Let's take a closer look at three important ones which are useful for part-time traders:

7. Optionable and shortable

Stocks which are 'optionable' offer the ability to trade shares for a set price at a specific time in the future. In my opinion, beginners should steer clear of options trading, because that's a part of the market which tends to produce a lot of sad stories. However, stocks which are optionable tend to be more liquid and this will stand to us when getting our orders filled.

As mentioned in the **Two Choices** chapter, shorting stocks has many advantages and this filter ensures there is a supply of shares available for shorting. Shortable stocks are also more liquid and it's no harm to have these in our watchlists to take advantage of short squeezes.

8. Volatility

Imagine a lie detector or a seismograph: low volatility is when the needle is barely moving, high volatility is when it's scratching furiously up and down. Volatility is the measure of how much a stock's price fluctuates over a given period of time. Essentially, how much the instrument moves up and down the price axis.

There is little point in trying to catch a strong move on a daily swing trade if the stock we are looking at hardly moves at all. On the other hand, we need stable stocks in our portfolio if we are going to hold them over a longer period. We can scan for volatility in a few ways, but I find **percent average true range (%ATR)** to be the best.

Average true range was first introduced in 1978 by Welles Wilder in his book, *New Concepts in Technical Trading Systems*.[8] The range of a stock

---

8   Welles, Wilder J., *New Concepts in Technical Trading Systems*, Trend Research 1978, ISBN-13: 978-0894590276.

refers to the height of a price bar and is calculated by subtracting the low of the bar from the high. True range goes one step further and includes the previous bar's closing price in the calculation. Average true range then applies an exponential moving average to a period of true ranges.

Percent ATR is obtained by dividing the ATR by the current price. We can start out with a %ATR scan of between 2–6%. This offers enough movement to trade without giving us whiplash.

9. Dividend yield

Many people invest in stocks just to receive regular dividend payments. When interest rates are low, solid and stable firms paying a decent dividend are attractive. For example, so-called 'sin stocks' (alcohol, tobacco, gambling and defense) tend to pay high dividends to encourage shareholder loyalty. Telecoms and real estate investment trusts (REITs) are also known as solid dividend payers. Some investors fill their portfolio with stocks paying a dividend each calendar month, so they receive a 'stock market salary'.

Traders can carry dividend payers in trend-following strategies and the extra few bucks are a nice top-up for gains already made on the trend. The dividend payments can also be very large. There is an urban myth among retail investors that stocks paying a high dividend are compensating for something and should be avoided. The facts tell a different story.

For example, a quick scan of the U.S. market with the following filters:[9]

- no ETFs

- optionable and shortable

- performance (rate of return) positive for past twelve months.

---

9 Finviz.com, Scanner, May 2018.

- net profit margin positive

- market cap > $2bn

- share price > $10

- average volume > 500,000

reveals four firms are paying a dividend in excess of 10% per year. That increases to 33 firms if we reduce the dividend to 5%, and 115 are paying more than 3%.

Obviously, we have no guarantee these firms will repeat this performance in the coming years, or maintain their dividend, but every year a sizable number of solid firms pay respectable dividends – we just have to find them.

It only takes a few minutes to visually scan through the charts of 115 stocks (a great mindfulness exercise), looking for unusual activity in the price history. This will reduce the list by a few names and we now have a good dividend-paying watchlist to work with.

When scanning for dividend-paying stocks we also need to consider cyclical stocks, which are seen as a 'luxury' and move in tandem with the economic cycle, while non-cyclical stocks are seen as a 'necessity' and tend to do better when times are tough. Non-cyclicals usually pay a good dividend and are seen as defensive (not to be confused with the aerospace and defense industry group).

Conclusion

As we scroll through the charts on our watchlist, we are looking for recognizable and tradable patterns. We should be so familiar with our favorite strategies that we can see at a glance if a chart has the necessary setup. This process is like going to meet an old friend at the airport. We visually scan through hundreds of strange faces but immediately spot our friend in the crowd because we are so accustomed to their appearance.

We should also keep an eye out for unusual trading activity in a stock's history. This might be a flash crash, regular price gaps or recurring spikes in volume. The price bars visible on our chart might look fine, but we should scroll to the left looking for skeletons in the stock's past.

When the filter is applied, a stock might make the list because it was a few pennies above the price or volume requirement. After two months, it might fall below the threshold but still be on the list. Therefore, we need to be familiar with our filter and manually remove any stock we see which no longer comes up to par. We shouldn't just blindly rely on our filter every three months – we need to be constantly vigilant for that one stock that can scuttle the ship.

TEN TOOLS

An Introduction to Technical Indicators and Orders

U P TO THIS point, we've looked at the psychology of
trading, risk management, trading procedures, records and
filters. Now it's time to take a closer look at the actual tools
we will use to extract money from the market.

There are numerous free websites which explain how every technical
indicator and trading order works, so there is little point in repeating
that here. Instead, I will identify those which I believe are underused
and underestimated but have stood the test of time. More to the point,
they have generated profits in the past and continue to do so today.

Five basic technical indicators

As traders we should use indicators in two ways – firstly to analyze the
market for trends, overbought or oversold conditions, reversal points,
participation and internal market activity not captured by popular

indices. Secondly, our indicators can be used to provide specific trading signals.

One of the biggest errors beginners make is to use too many technical indicators. A minimalist approach to the subject is best because every financial instrument oscillates inside a channel, which in turn meanders up and down the chart. We just need the basics to measure this simultaneous movement.

1. Price action

Price can be interpreted in two ways: **price action** and **price location**. Price action refers to the shapes and forms created by price bars and how this captures the dynamic of **effort and reward**, in addition to **supply and demand**. Price location is the position of the current price relative to its history, and this can be examined with the use of moving averages which we cover next.

By closely watching the price, we can get an accurate gauge of the market's true feelings. Trading and investing in shares is essentially a continuous public vote where individual shareholders express their view on the future prospects of the company. The current price is the real-time result of the votes cast so far.

The seven basic numbers

Everything we see on our charts has been calculated from just seven numbers – time, date, open, high, low, close and volume. These are the seeds from which all the colorful technical indicators blossom. With these seven, we can create any momentum indicator or oscillator, we can backtest as far as we have data, and we can create any chart we wish.

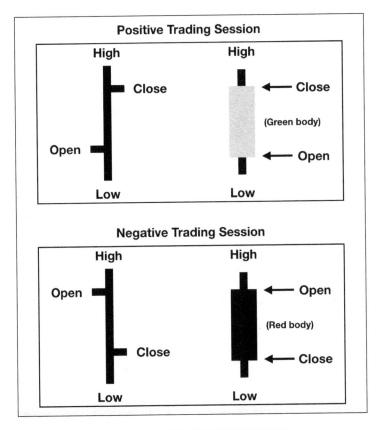

FIGURE 19: PRICE BARS AND CANDLESTICKS

In order to capture this action, we need to use open-high-low-close (OHLC) bars or candlesticks. The latter tend to be the tool of choice for new traders and we have all memorized the 'most important' candlestick patterns. Evening stars, hanging men, abandoned babies and dojis, to name but a few. When we spot one of these exotic candlestick formations, we should remember, *so has everyone else*. Therefore, entering a trade on the basis of price action alone can be a highly risky strategy and is more suited to scalping and day trading.

The opening of each trading session is like an opening night on Broadway. The nerves, the excitement and the optimism when the market bell rings are all reduced to a number which we call 'open'. As the euphoria and excess of the day reaches its peak, it becomes 'high'. Pessimism and fear hit the depths of depression at their 'low'. And finally, when all the drama is over, participants accept their fate and bring closure to the session as they settle for the 'close'. Therefore, the closing price is the most important price of the day.

Reversals and price washouts

When filling orders, the market is like a shoal of hungry fish, frantically swimming back and forth eating every order it sees. When all the orders in front of it have been consumed, it turns around on itself and goes looking for orders in the opposite direction. By closely watching these price reversals during the day, and the strength of the move after the reversal, we have a strong indication of where most of the orders are sitting.

Experienced traders wait for this price action to trigger them into a trade: they don't jump the gun. It's like buying a condo off-plan. If we wait until the foundations have been laid before investing, there is a higher probability the building will be completed. It might cost a little more to buy into the stock after the move has begun, but the slight reduction in reward more than compensates for the large reduction in risk.

Automated (or conditional) orders are an excellent way to do this. These orders will only execute when a pre-defined set of conditions have occurred in sequence. For example, many swing trading strategies are highly dependent on price action and some of them can be as simple as entering on a price 'washout' and when moving average lines cross over.

A washout occurs when the price drops to a level which is lower than the previous day's low (the lower the better), reverses and closes higher than the previous day's close. Only when this has happened, will the automated order trigger.

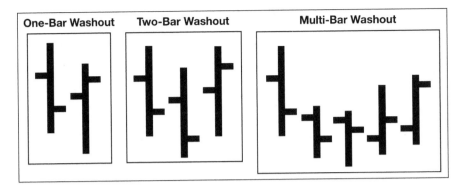

FIGURE 20: ONE-BAR WASHOUT (1BW), TWO-BAR WASHOUT (2BW) AND MULTI-BAR WASHOUT (MBW)

This can happen in one-price bar – a one-bar washout (1BW) – or two price bars – a two-bar washout (2BW). A 1BW is the strongest reversal signal, as the market reversed in just one price-bar interval – it took just one basketball to trigger all the mousetraps. A 2BW is also valid because it's the same thing, but just took a little longer. A multi-bar washout (MBW) is a messy affair and we are best to avoid this type of price action for entries.

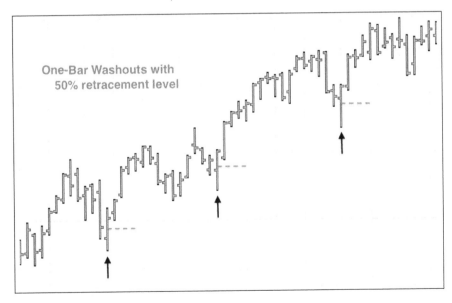

FIGURE 21: ONE-BAR WASHOUTS AND 50% RETRACEMENT LEVELS

In the case of a good 1BW, the follow-up price action shouldn't trade back below half the range (height) of the trigger bar, so I place a soft stop at about a 60% retracement of the bar. The same soft stop can be applied to a 2BW, using the low of the first bar and the high of the second bar to calculate the retracement level.

These washout, reversal and retracement stop levels also apply to short trades, except in reverse, where we calculate from the highs of the price bars rather than the lows.

Washouts are important because they clear the air and settle the current disagreement between bulls and bears. The more powerful group pushes deep into the territory of the weaker one, crushing the resistance it encountered at the border. Flushed with victory, they grab their spoils and turn around and take the market in their direction, with no one to oppose them.

2. Moving average – price and value

I once shared a five-star hotel room with an alcoholic. He was at a point in his drinking career where he had managed to hide his drinking from nobody but himself. During the night he emptied all the bottles in the minibar and filled them with water from the tap. When we went to check out, the eagle-eyed staff had spotted the broken seals on the bottles and a hefty bill was waiting for us.

As the awkward situation unfolded, I was shocked to discover the hotel were charging more for one tiny bottle of vodka from the minibar than the price of a full bottle in a liquor store. Driving away from the hotel, I realized we had just been given a valuable lesson in the difference between price and value.

Price is what something sells for, value is what it's actually worth. In the minibar, price is always above value because of the convenient location of the little bottles and the lack of discipline of the guests. In the financial markets, price and value weave above and below each other as the market moves forward. This creates opportunities for traders to profit.

Buying shares when they are overvalued is drinking from the minibar; when they are undervalued we are getting the stuff from the distillery. There is always a party around the minibar because that's where the cool crowd hang out, whereas the distillery is in a lonely industrial park on the edge of town. On our journey of discovery as traders, we need to avoid the temptations of the minibar crowd and keep our cash dry for the distillery.

Before we place a single penny in a stock, we need to understand how the location of the current price relates to value. Is the stock over-valued, under-valued or just about right? We could do this by looking at the **price-to-earnings ratio** (P/E) and its historical context or by trawling through the company financials. A much easier method is to stick a **moving average** line on a chart.

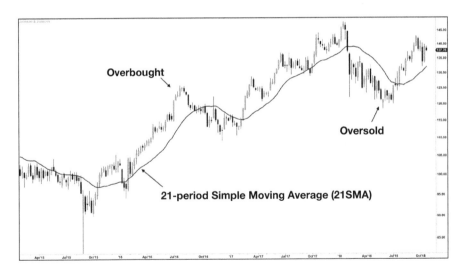

FIGURE 22: 21-PERIOD SIMPLE MOVING AVERAGE LINE (21SMA) ON A WEEKLY CHART OF JOHNSON & JOHNSON (NYSE:JNJ)

This is when we calculate the average share price for a fixed period in time and then advance one step and do the calculation again. Each time we add a new figure at one end and drop one at the other end. We plot the results on a chart in the form of a continuous line and overlay it on the share price. We should plot this line good and thick. After price, this is probably the single most important piece of information available to traders.

There are two types of moving average: **simple** and **exponential**. A simple moving average (SMA) assigns equal value to every data point when doing the calculation. But the markets are not that simple, so traders also use an exponential moving average (EMA) which applies a slight weighting to the more recent data. This smooths the curve and alerts us sooner to a trend change.

The amount of data used to calculate the moving average will depend on the particular strategy we are trading, but a 21-period exponential moving average calculated from the closing prices (21EMAC) is a good place to start. On a daily chart, this is the past 21 days, which is about a month's trading, so any fluctuations based on month-end transactions will be captured. On a weekly chart, a 21EMAC represents about half a year, so seasonal variations and two earnings reports should be covered. On a monthly chart, we are covering nearly two years of data, but we also get an overview of the important 200-month cycles which are found in the market.

FIGURE 23: 21SMA AND 21EMAC ON A DAILY CHART OF ALPHABET
(GOOGLE) (NASDAQ: GOOGL)

A 21EMAC line is also ideal for identifying trends. We should save a
chart specifically for that purpose. Whenever we are unsure about the
market, a weekly chart with a 21EMAC on it will remind us which
way the trend is going. They say, 'The trend is your friend' – and the
weekly 21EMAC will keep us in touch with this influential ally.

FIGURE 24: 12EMAC AND 21EMAC ON A WEEKLY CHART OF TESLA
(NASDAQ: TSLA) SHOWING 'VALUE ZONE'

For trading purposes, some people use two moving averages of different lengths. On more than one occasion, I have heard Dr. Alexander Elder say, "Value lives in the zone between the two moving averages." This 'value zone' is what the stock is currently worth, and the location of the price relative to it shows if the stock is currently oversold or overbought.

On a daily chart, the fast-moving average should be a figure in the low teens such as 11–12 and the slow-moving average should be in the low twenties, 21–23. We shouldn't get hung up on the exact figures. If the slow EMA is about twice the length of the fast one, they are doing the job required.

We can think of the fast and slow EMAs as an 18-wheeler tractor trailer unit. As the truck moves forward, the tractor unit (fast EMA) will make tighter shorter curves and respond quicker, while the trailer unit (slow EMA) will follow in wider, looser turns. Both sets of wheels leave their print on the ground while following a slightly different path.

The value zone is one of the first things we should look for when considering a trade. The P/E simply doesn't come into it and I am unaware of any traders who consider it when placing trades.

Most beginners are trend followers or swing traders whether they realize it or not. They are either following a trend on the long side or swing trading against the trend – or doing a bit of both. They should know where value is before attempting these strategies, because they are all based on the convergence or divergence of price and value. If they don't know where value is, how do they know where to start?

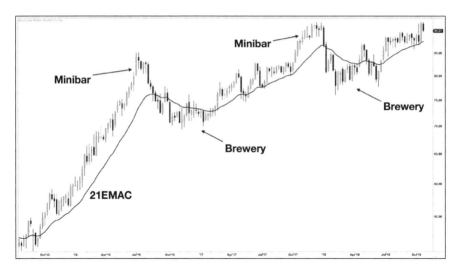

FIGURE 25: PRICE AND VALUE (MINIBAR AND BREWERY) ON A WEEKLY CHART OF AMERICAN WATER WORKS (NYSE: AWK)

For a trend follower, the idea is to get in when the price is below value and hunker down for the long haul as the price continues to climb. Swing traders try to catch a move from an overbought or oversold condition, which can last a few days or a week. In both cases, they are looking to buy below value and sell at or above value. (Obviously when trading short the opposite applies.) Having established where value is using an EMA, they now have a reference point for entries and exits.

By default, most charting packages use the closing price of each trading period to calculate the moving average. More advanced packages allow us to use any one of the four significant price points during a trading period (open, high, low and close).

The 50-day and 200-day simple moving averages (SMA) are frequently used by large institutions to identify trend changes. It's always good to know what the big boys are doing, because they are like a heavy guy in a small boat – when he moves, everything moves.

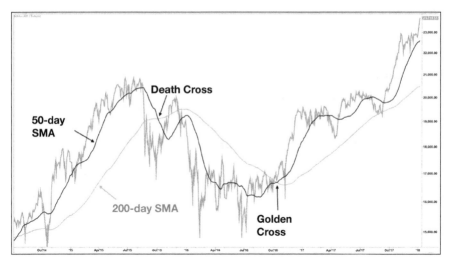

FIGURE 26: DAILY CHART OF NIKKEI 225 INDEX SHOWING 50-DAY SMA
AND 200-DAY SMA CROSSOVERS

When the faster-changing 50-day SMA crosses the 200-day SMA from below, they call it a **golden cross** – because the trend is changing to the upside and things are looking golden. When the opposite occurs, it's called a **death cross** as the trend has turned to the downside and things are looking terminal. When these crossovers occur, they can add fuel to the progress of the market.

A very useful exercise is to pull up a chart of some stocks we are currently holding or watching and plot a 21EMAC on it. Look back along the chart and notice how the EMA and price always seek each other out and continuously reunite. Regardless of whether the trend is up or down, price and value always come back together.

Now highlight on the chart where you opened and closed positions. Did you get a bargain or did you pay too much? Also, take note of where the trend changed direction. A common mistake among beginners is to buy just before the top and sell just before the market bottoms out. It's as if their order changed the market direction.

Using moving average as a guide to value has kept me out of trouble more times than I care to remember. Those little minibar bottles were expensive at the time but have proven to be a cheap lesson in hindsight.

3. Average true range (ATR) channels[1]

Stocks fluctuate up and down as they move along the chart, but healthy stocks stay inside a channel, like a sober pedestrian stays on a footpath. Average true range (ATR) channels take the concept of a moving average line representing value one step further, by measuring the average height of a series of price bars (volatility) based around a moving average line.

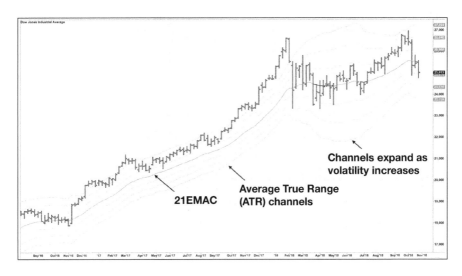

FIGURE 27: WEEKLY CHART OF DOW JONES INDUSTRIAL AVERAGE ($INDU) WITH THREE AVERAGE TRUE RANGE (ATR) CHANNELS

ATR channels define the width of a stock's footpath and allow us to gauge the recent volatility of a stock at a glance and also provide levels to locate protective stops and targets. We can also use them to determine the extent of overbought and oversold conditions. Simply

---

1   StockCharts – Keltner Channels (stockcharts.com/school/doku.php?id=chart_school:technical_indicators:keltner_channels).

put, when we know what the average range of a stock price is, we can spot when the price is doing something out of the ordinary and respond accordingly.

Kerry Lovvorn is a strong proponent of ATR channels and he introduced me to the concept. In fact, they are such a comprehensive and useful tool, I use them in one form or another on almost all my charts these days. Typically, three equidistant ATR channels are plotted above and below a central 21EMAC line. For the most part, stocks stay inside the top and bottom third channels, and major market indices rarely move outside them.

In price action above, we looked at price washouts – ATR channels can also be used in this regard. A 'good washout' should be at least 0.25ATR below the recent lows of the price bars.

4. Volume

Different methods of measurement are used for volume. Some exchanges count the number of transactions (ticks) and some count the number of shares traded. We should know which is used on the exchange we are trading. Most of the time, volume doesn't tell us anything on its own. It is used to confirm the conviction or sentiment in a move. It confirms how much weight is behind a push or pullback and how eager the buyers and sellers are to trade at certain levels.

Just as a sentence or phrase can give the wrong impression when used out of context, volume must be understood in terms of what's going on in the market at the time.

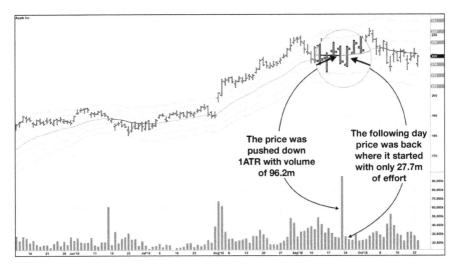

FIGURE 28: EFFORT AND REWARD ON A DAILY CHART OF APPLE
(NASDAQ: AAPL)

Volume and price when viewed together give us an indication of effort
and reward. How much effort (volume) was required to move the
price, and how far did it go (reward) with that effort. It also gives an
insight into the all-important dynamic of supply and demand. We can
measure the appetite of the market as supply and demand increases or
decreases at a certain price level.

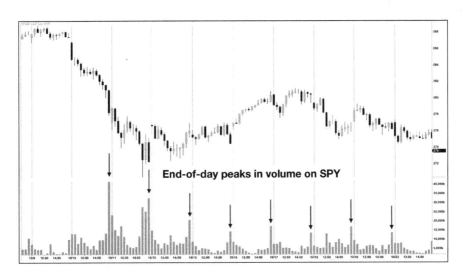

FIGURE 29: END-OF-DAY PEAKS IN VOLUME ON A 30MIN CHART OF
SPDR® S&P 500® ETF

There is often a spike in volume at the end of a trading period, as profits are taken or unprofitable trades are closed out. If we are trading a weekly chart, it's good practice to drop down to a daily chart and see how volume is distributed throughout the week. Likewise, we can pull up an intraday chart to get a handle on volume during the day.

5. Support and resistance (S/R)

That sounds like a recruiting slogan for a militant political group, but it's actually a method for identifying established levels in the market. These are horizontal zones where falling prices find a floor (support), and reverse or rising prices appear to hit a ceiling (resistance) and fall back. This happens because market players made previous commitments at these price levels (both mentally and with actual orders) and the pledges now fall due. When the market revisits these levels, participants are inclined to buy or sell depending on previous experience.

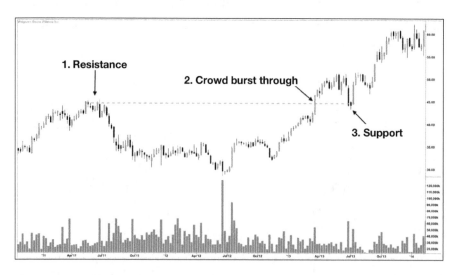

FIGURE 30: SUPPORT AND RESISTANCE LEVELS ON WEEKLY CHART OF WALGREEN BOOTS ALLIANCE (NASDAQ: WBA)

Support and resistance work like swinging doors. When a crowd pushes lightly against the doors they give a little and a few people might get through, but the doors push back and keep the crowd out. The force of the crowd has to be strong enough to burst through the doors. Once they eventually get through, the doors swing shut behind them and they will have to apply similar force to get back out again. Previous resistance becomes support and visa versa.

Just as every good soccer player knows where the sideline and goal line is, we should always know the location of the short-, medium- and long-term support and resistance zones for the positions we are trading. Long-term zones can be found using a monthly chart, medium-term levels with a weekly chart and short-term zones will be obvious on a daily chart.

To identify the zones, we should look for levels where opening and closing prices are clustered, rather than the extremes of the price bars. Because of the nature of these zones, there is a degree of interpretation involved. It's almost as if a mood or feeling exists at the levels, rather than there being a figure set in stone.

People tend to get anxious if the conversation drifts onto a sensitive subject; likewise when the market enters a support and resistance zone, traders get edgy.

We think of support and resistance in terms of zones rather than specific levels or numbers because they are like big spongy doors which absorb a lot of pushing and jostling before they eventually crack open. Remember, these zones are clusters of orders, so the zone flexes a little as the market frantically runs up and down filling those orders.

Breakout

Support and resistance zones are often tested a few times before the market crowd can burst through. The more times the doors withstand a push, the stronger we know they are. Eventually when the doors are breached, the effort which was required to get through can be so strong that the crowd flood through and the move continues. This is called a **breakout** and is a very popular trading strategy, especially among beginners.

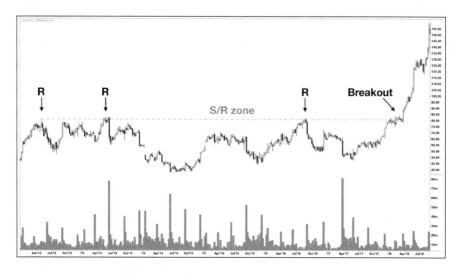

FIGURE 31: BREAKOUT ON A WEEKLY CHART OF LULULEMON ATHLETICA (NASDAQ: LULU) AFTER THREE ATTEMPTS

False breakout

But we need to be careful with breakouts. The price can often get through the zone for a few hours or days but then falls back. This is known as a **false breakout** and means only a few traders got through the doors, but the crowd were not convinced by the move and stopped pushing. In this case, the few who did manage to get through are now isolated on the wrong side of market opinion.

FIGURE 32: FALSE AND CONFIRMED BREAKOUTS ON A DAILY CHART OF PFIZER (NYSE: PFE)

A breakout is only confirmed when price tests the support and resistance doors from the other side and they hold firm. False breakouts are a popular strategy among professionals, as they trade against all the breakout alerts previously set by amateurs. The long wick on a false breakout candle is like a lightning rod for beginners. Electrified with enthusiasm, they are drawn to the spike – only to be brought down to earth by the market.

Average true range support and resistance (ATR S/R)

Support and resistance zones don't just exist on horizontal levels, they also manifest in terms of volatility. ATR channels can be used to identify these levels for swing trading because stocks oscillate inside their ATR channel. A rising stock will often reverse as it encounters an ATR line (especially the 3ATR line) and a falling stock will frequently encounter support at the -1 or -2ATR line.

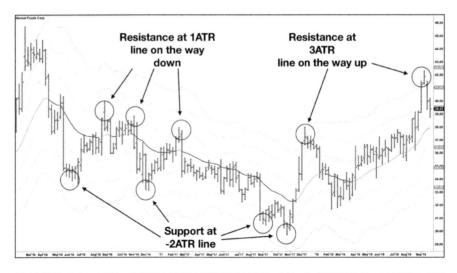

FIGURE 33: ATR SUPPORT/RESISTANCE ON A WEEKLY CHART OF HORMEL FOODS (NYSE: HRL)

FIGURE 34: DAILY CHART OF ANHEUSER-BUSCH INBEV (NYSE: BUD) OSCILLATING INSIDE ITS CHANNEL UNTIL IT BREAKS DOWN

Volume at price support and resistance (Vol S/R)

Volume and price can be combined in a single indicator known as **volume at price**. Like rubble stacked on the battlefield, this indicator shows where most of the trading action took place by measuring the volume of transactions at each price level. The dual nature of the indicator is especially useful for confirming the strength of support and resistance zones and how the market might react when it returns to these levels. Volume at price identifies the most intense struggles between bulls and bears.

When volume at price S/R levels overlap with their horizontal and ATR counterparts, it's a serious level to be reckoned with and extra attention is warranted.

The limitation of technical analysis

Technical analysis of the financial markets is an historical mathematical measure of a live emotional event. Accordingly, when we fixate on the numbers, we can miss the point entirely.

Mary and Patrick have been engaged for five years. One evening as they sit watching TV, Mary turns to Pat and asks, "Do you love me?" Pat, who is a technical analyst, instinctively replies, "Of course I love you." Encouraged by that answer, she snuggles closer and says, "Well I know you love me, but how much do you love me?" Judging by the tone in her voice Pat knows the question is important, so he contemplates his answer for a moment and finally replies, "Mary, I love you 1.2% more than the last time you asked me!"

Five basic orders

We can all remember the spoiled kid who lived up the street. He would only engage with others on his terms and refuse to play along unless he got his way. We should follow his example and do exactly the same with the market. Many new traders don't realize they can pick and choose the type of orders they use. Rather than just jumping in with an order to buy or sell, we can tell the market what we want and refuse to play along unless we get it.

Let's examine a few of the common orders used by traders:

1. Market order

The stock market is the world's greatest online auction and speed-dating event, all rolled into one. If you have attended one of these prestigious gatherings, you know you need to have your wits about you. This is especially true for traders because we are trying to make a living out of them.

A **market order** is an order to trade regardless of the price and takes no account of what's sitting in front of us. That is never a good idea in any forum. Placing a market order is like saying to the market, '*Buy 1,000 shares!*' and the market asks, '*How would you like me to execute that order, sir?*' and you reply, '*Ah sure, whatever you think yourself.*' The market is always thinking about itself, not about us. For this reason, market orders should rarely be used.

Having said that, protective stops are market orders. It's not a perfect solution, but it's the best we have and trading liquid stocks will ensure market stop loss orders are filled quickly.

2. Limit order

As the name suggests, a **limit order** sets a limit on how much we are prepared to pay. The order sits on our broker's server and will only trigger when the price trades at the level we have set. On occasion the price can jump over a limit order and run away without us, but the advantages of a limit order far outweigh the downside. Most orders we use when trading should be limit orders.

3. Stop-limit order

A **stop-limit order** is a two-part order which will only trigger if the stock trades between two prices. For example, if we are trading long (buying) and have a buy-stop order at $90 and a stop-limit at $91.50, then the order will only execute when the price trades above $90, but will not pay more than $91.50. These orders are especially good for catching reversal moves. They trigger us into a trade only after all the orders stacked in the opposite direction have been washed out. Then the market can only go one way and we are going with it.

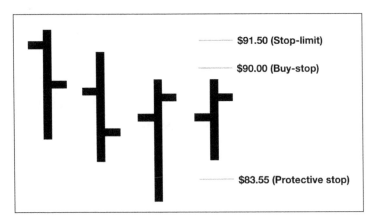

FIGURE 35: STOP-LIMIT ORDER

4. Protective stop – the most important order of all

In July 1985, Hersh Shefrin and Meir Statman at the University of Santa Clara in California confirmed what successful traders have always known. They published a paper in *The Journal of Finance* entitled, 'The Disposition to Sell Winners Too Early and Ride Losers Too Long: Theory and Evidence.'[2] They referred to this common behavior among traders and investors as the "disposition effect".

How exactly do we know when a loss has to be cut? At what point has it become a loser? As for winners, how do we let them run and for how long? In the market, long-term winners can be losers for short periods and losers can start out as winners. The solution to the conundrum and the cure for the disposition effect is a **protective stop**.

2   Hersh Shefrin and Meir Statman, 'The Disposition to Sell Winners Too Early and Ride Losers Too Long: Theory and Evidence', *The Journal of Finance*, vol. 40, no. 3, Papers and Proceedings of the Forty-Third Annual Meeting American Finance Association, Dallas, Texas, 28–30 December 1984 (Jul., 1985), pp.777-790. www.jstor. org/stable/2327802?seq=1#page_scan_tab_contents.

A protective stop is the most important tool in our box – it's as relevant to a trader as a sword is to a gladiator or a microphone is to a comedian.

We already looked at protective stops in the **Two Choices** chapter, but there are two types of protective stop: a **hard stop** and a **soft stop**. A hard stop is when we place a live order to close our position when the stock trades at a certain price. A soft stop (also known as a **mental stop**) is a figure we have in our head, where we will close out the trade if the price reaches that level. That's fine in theory, but soft stops should be avoided by beginners because it's a test of discipline they may not possess.

Think of it this way: a fella goes to the pub after work on Friday. A soft stop is when he takes his wage packet with him and tells himself he will come home after two pints. A hard stop is when he only takes the price of two pints and arranges for his wife and her mother to pick him up at nine o' clock.

The first cut is the shallowest   •

Cat Stevens wrote the love song, 'The First Cut is the Deepest.' Every time we hear this song, we should remember emotions have no place in the market. A protective stop inflicts the first cut in our equity and it's actually the shallowest, not the deepest. It cuts us free from a bigger loss. The sooner we take the first cut the better. Small cuts heal quickly, and the market will always give us more opportunities – it won't always give us more capital.

When good traders are stopped out of a trade, they perk up and watch the stock even more closely because they know the trade frequently offers a better trigger soon afterwards. Once they know the setup is good, they keep trying to get a good entry. A protective stop is the point where they accept they were wrong on this occasion but might be right soon afterwards.

There is no feeling of upset or regret on their part. They are relaxed because they know they arrived to the party a little earlier than everyone else and can now pick the best seat in the house. It's common for professionals to enter a trade too early; beginners enter too late.

We should think of protective stops as a trading strategy which moves us from one asset to another, rather than an annoyance or a necessary evil. They automatically trigger us out of a position in equities which is turning against us and into a position in cash which is always a good place to be. When a stop is triggered, we should never see it as a failure on our part.

Location of protective stops

A common question posed by new traders is where to place their protective stops. This decision should never be made in isolation and should be just one element of a trading strategy. When placing a trade, we should already know the location of our stops and possible 'targets' and send these orders into the market simultaneously.

This is known as a **bracket order**, because we place connected orders above and below the current price. Ideally all orders should be part of an overall bracket order. Not only does this offer us maximum protection, but it forces us to consider the risk/reward profile of the trade.

Volatility (ATR)-based protective stops

The reasoning behind volatility-based stops comes from the idea we should place our stops outside the average range of movement of a stock for the time frame we are trading. Common sense would indicate we will be stopped out of the position by normal market noise if our stops are inside the average range of the stock. When the price moves outside its average range, it strays from its footpath and walks into oncoming traffic.

The use of volatility-based protective stops has been around for a while and was an integral part of the trading system used by the famous

Turtle Traders[3] in the 1980s. I find volatility-based stops to be the most effective and profitable type of protective stop. In **Part C** we will see an example of ATR-volatility-based stops in action.

5. Trailing stop

Selling winners too early is the other bad habit identified by Shefrin and Statman. The solution to this is a **trailing stop**. This is a protective stop which we move as the trade progresses in order to preserve the profits made so far. Once the price starts to go in our direction, we 'trail' our protective stop behind it, little by little so as to lock in as much profit as possible without increasing our risk. When the trend ends and the price whips back at us, the trailing stop kicks us into cash with most of the profit in our pocket.

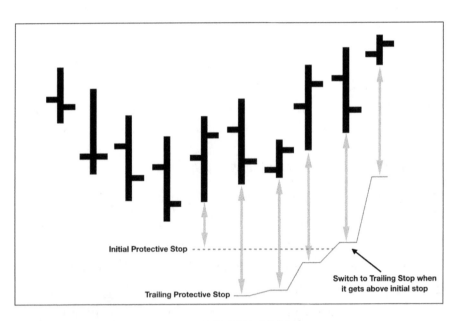

Initial Protective Stop

Trailing Protective Stop

Switch to Trailing Stop when it gets above initial stop

FIGURE 36: TRAILING STOP ON A RISING STOCK

---

3   The Original Turtle Trading Rules, © 2003 OriginalTurtles.org, p.22 (www. tradingblox.com/originalturtles/originalturtlerules.htm).

A trailing stop really earns its keep when a position we are holding goes into a parabolic climb. This is when the price just goes straight up like a rocket and all common sense is left smoldering on the launch pad. At this point, most of our technical indicators are rendered useless because their calculations are drawn from a look-back window which has yet to incorporate the sudden jump in price.

Where to place a trailing stop

For trend followers, the location of a trailing stop is crucial because that's the main thing we will be monitoring as the trade unfolds. When we are sitting in a trade for weeks or months, watching the price approach and reverse from our trailing stop, there is enormous temptation to move it. So, we have to be 100% comfortable with the location we choose.

This is directly related to our preference for whipsaw or lag – yet again we are back to the **Two Choices** of trading. A tight stop (one which is close to the current price) is more likely to be hit and generate whipsaws. A loose stop (one which is farther away from the price) will give the trade more time to work out, but results in a smaller position size, and smaller profit.

Fine-tuning protective stops

For years I played around with the location of protective stops, searching for the optimum level which extracted the maximum profit. When I went back over all my trades in a systematic manner, calculating what the profits and losses would have been with various stop locations, something much more important than stop location came to light.

I frequently missed re-entries after whipsaws and in the process missed great trades, because I stopped monitoring the stocks on my watchlist and went chasing after something else. Potential profits of 15 or 20% were always lost in this way, whereas fine-tuning stop levels would have increased the profit by just one or two per cent.

Mary couldn't care less if Patrick loves her 1.2% more or 2.2% more; splitting hairs about percentages completely misses the point. Likewise the money in trading is made from generosity, discipline, patience, diligence, concentration and wisdom – not by fine-tuning stop levels.

PART
C

THE STRATEGIES

Perfect Imperfection

EW DIAMONDS ARE perfect. They all come out of the ground with imperfections on the inside. Dealers refer to these marks as 'inclusions', whereas retail jewelers describe them to their customers as 'unique characteristics'. Just like diamonds, all trading strategies have unique characteristics and we need to accept this facet of trading if we are to succeed.

Experienced traders know the 'imperfection' in a profitable trading strategy is the very thing which makes it perfect. If a strategy worked all the time, everyone would use it and it would cease to be profitable. If it works most of the time and its unique characteristics frustrate the majority of traders – then it's a perfect strategy.

A diamond is brought to life only when it's cut and polished, and that requires skill. In the following chapters, I will share three rough-diamond strategies which have made money in the past and are still generating profits today. These strategies are not profitable 100% of the time, because such a strategy does not exist. However, if you are ready to work with strategies which consistently offer profitable opportunities, they are a good place to hone your skills.

Signals and triggers

As we saw in the **Four Legs** chapter, we should never enter a trade without a series of **signals** being present – like dials on a combination lock. In the following strategies, we will see how a **trigger** occurs when the required signals are present, and we proceed with a pre-defined action. This can be the process of entering or exiting the trade at our discretion or with a mechanical approach.

Backtested results

There is no shortage of people hawking trading strategies and claiming amazing results as they take selfies in their sports car. Not surprisingly, they never provide real life backtested data for these elusive money makers. Most of these strategies are also discretionary, where the seller can pick and choose trades which suit their narrative – and usually after the event.

In my experience, the best traders have no more than five or six strategies and frequently trade just two or three on a regular basis. Two of the strategies which follow are mechanical and I have included comprehensive backtested results for both – make up your own mind.

THE TIDAL
STRATEGY

Introduction

THE TIDAL STRATEGY is a mechanical long-only monthly trend-following strategy which takes advantage of a market tide which has turned to the upside and reverts to cash when the tide starts going out. It can be used in any large, developed and well-regulated equity market where a diversified index is accurately tracked by a highly liquid and low-cost ETF.

This strategy is close to the investing end of the spectrum, but I refer to it as a trade because we use technical indicators rather than market fundamentals to inform our entry and exit decisions. It's also an excellent way for beginners to make the transition to trading.

SPY

The SPDR® S&P 500® ETF (NYSE:SPY) from State Street Global Advisors is probably the most well-known ETF in the markets and has been around for nearly a quarter of a century (us.spdrs.com/en/etf/spdr-sp-500-etf-SPY). It closely tracks the performance of the S&P 500 index as it holds the same 500 firms used to calculate the index. It is regularly the most actively traded instrument in the US markets, so there is no issue with liquidity.

Other well-known ETFs which track the S&P 500 index are:

- iShares (NYSE: IVV) – www.ishares.com/us/literature/fact-sheet/ivv-ishares-core-s-p-500-etf-fund-fact-sheet-en-us.pdf

- Vanguard (NYSE: VOO) – institutional.vanguard.com/iippdf/pdfs/FS968R.pdf

I used SPY to demonstrate the Tidal Strategy as it offers the most historic data, but any S&P 500 ETF with a low expense ratio can be used. According to State Street's factsheet, it "seeks to provide investment results that, before expenses, correspond generally to the price and yield performance of the S&P500® Index."

Prior to 1993, private traders and investors with small accounts would have been unable to gain direct access to such a diversified portfolio of stocks via an inexpensive fund. ETFs now make this possible for everyone.

Indicators

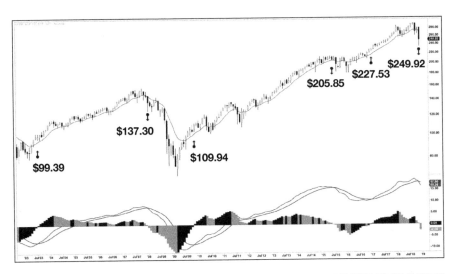

FIGURE 37: TIDAL STRATEGY ON A MONTHLY CHART OF SPDR® S&P 500®
ETF (NYSE: SPY) 2002–2018

This strategy is really simple, because we get our trigger from just two signals – monthly price candles (or bars) and a moving average convergence divergence histogram (**MACD-H**).

(a) Monthly price candles

We plot SPY on a monthly chart using candlesticks set to a semi-log scale. 'Semi-log' is scaled on percentage change, whereas 'linear' scales on absolute price. Semi-log gets more on a monthly chart because the change in price over time can be large.

(b) Moving average convergence divergence histogram (MACD-H)[1]

This is a wonderful tool as it has properties of both a momentum indicator and an oscillator. MACD-H displays two exponential

---

1   Appel, Gerald, *Technical Analysis Power Tools for Active Investors*, Financial Times Prentice-Hall 2005, ISBN 0-13-147902-4.

moving average lines and a bar graph (histogram) of how these relate to their nine-period EMA.

Under the candles, we plot a MACD-H and this will provide our primary signal. The most popular settings for MACD-H are 12, 26, 9 – where 12 and 26 are the moving average lengths. However, I find moving average lines set at 18 and 36 strike a good balance between whipsaw and lag on a monthly chart of SPY. There is enough lag not to be triggered out by a short-term correction, while they are tight enough to respond quickly to a bear market.

Signals

We open a position (or stay long) when the histogram bar for the current month closes above the zero line on the last trading day in the month. When the histogram closes below the zero line, we close the position or stay in cash – it's as simple as that!

It is imperative we wait for the last day of the month to make our decision. The close of a monthly candle stamps a definitive line on the chart as accounts are settled and investment performance is calculated. In addition, the end of every third month coincides with the end of a quarter, so we should wait for all market participants to reveal their hand.

Protective stop

The zero line on the histogram will act as our soft stop-loss order, on a monthly closing basis. We don't use a hard stop because SPY is such a liquid instrument and the market can experience pullbacks and corrections during a month before resuming the original trend.

Backtesting

Chart	Entry Date	Entry Price	Exit Date	Exit Price	Months	Gain (Loss) %
			SPY (MACD-H Signals)			
INX	30-Apr-63	6.98	30-Jul-65	8.53	27	22.21
INX	29-Oct-65	9.24	31-Mar-66	8.92	5	-3.46
INX	30-Jun-67	9.06	29-Mar-68	9.02	9	-0.49
INX	30-Apr-68	9.87	30-Jun-69	9.77	14	-0.98
INX	29-Jan-71	9.59	31-May-73	10.50	28	9.46
INX	30-May-75	9.12	31-May-77	9.61	25	5.45
INX	31-Aug-78	10.33	31-Nov-78	9.47	3	-8.32
INX	31-Jan-79	9.99	30-Sep-81	11.62	32	16.26
INX	30-Nov-82	13.85	30-Apr-84	16.01	17	15.53
INX	31-Jan-85	17.96	30-Nov-87	23.03	34	28.21
INX	28-Apr-89	30.96	30-Apr-90	33.08	12	6.84
INX	30-Apr-91	37.54	30-Oct-92	41.87	18	11.54
INX	30-Nov-92	43.14	28-Feb-94	46.71	15	8.30
SPY	28-Apr-95	51.47	31-May-00	142.81	61	177.46
SPY	31-Jul-03	99.39	31-Jan-08	137.30	54	38.14
SPY	30-Nov-09	109.94	30-Jun-15	205.85	67	87.24
SPY	31-Jan-17	227.53	31-Dec-18	249.92	23	9.84
				Average	26	24.89%

FIGURE 38: SPREADSHEET OF BACKTESTED RESULTS OF THE TIDAL STRATEGY (1963–2018)

It's easy to backtest a strategy. Backtesting a trader's mind and their ability to apply it diligently over decades is another matter entirely. Notwithstanding this fact, we can see this strategy performed exceptionally well for the past 55 years.

Over the period tested (30 April 1963 to 31 December 2018) I used SPY from 22 January 1993 onwards and the cash index of the S&P 500 prior to that (adjusted by one tenth to correlate with SPY). Over the 55 years tested, the market had some serious declines, but this strategy avoided the worst of them while taking advantage of the gains.

For example, the S&P 500 dropped 49.92% from a peak in January 1973 to the bear market bottom in October 1974. From March 2000 to October 2002, it lost 50.5%, and in the 2008 crash it dropped 57.7%

from October 2007 to March 2009. On those three occasions, the largest drawdown on this strategy was just 8.32%.

The shortest time spent in cash was just a month, which occurred twice – in 1968 and 1992 – whereas the longest period in cash was over three years. On the other hand, the longest time spent in a position was five and a half years. Coincidentally (or maybe not), the average time spent in a position was 26 months and the average gain was almost 25%.

The exit in November 1987 was triggered by Black Monday on 19 October, which saw a 34.2% drop in the market. That would have been a very difficult period for anyone trading a strategy like this, but the position gave a profit of 28.21% since the entry was in January 1985.

The period November 1992 (Black Wednesday in the U.K.) to February 1994 would also have been a particularly difficult time. The signal regularly flirted with the zero line but just managed to close above it each time, until it eventually signalled an exit in early 1994.

The Russian currency devaluation and debt default in August 1998 very nearly triggered a signal but the histogram managed to stay above the zero line by 0.39 points in September and October and the bull market continued for another two years. I clearly recall the doom and gloom and talk of the impending collapse of the global financial order. Thankfully, capitalism recovered from its near-death experience and the strategy went on to catch most of the bull market, with a profit of 177.46% when it exited before the dotcom bubble burst.

Dividends and trading expenses

SPY paid a quarterly dividend of 0.613% on 24 December 2018.[2] When compounded, this is a significant bonus over time. Ideally, we will

---

2   A dividend of $1.435429 will be paid on 31 January 2019 for the record date of 24 December 2018 when SPY closed at $234.34

have sufficient funds in our account to avoid monthly account charges from our broker and the cost of trading should be no more than $5 each time. Regardless of our position size, the dividends should be more than enough to cover expenses, but neither were included in the backtested results.

Sell in May?

Some unusual patterns are observed when we examine which months of the year signals occurred. Should we 'sell in May and go away' as some suggest? The entry in May 1975 produced a gain of 5.45% by the time it exited two years later – in May. The entry on the last day of April 1989 gave us a 6.84% profit when it exited a year later – on the last day of April. The following April (1991) we entered a trade which resulted in 11.54% profit over 18 months. The best trade over the 55-year period entered in April and exited in May.

Life before SPY

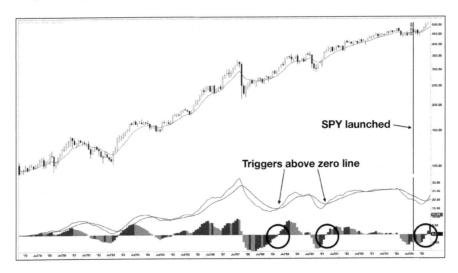

FIGURE 39: ABOVE THE ZERO LINE RE-ENTRY TRIGGERS ON S&P 500 INDEX (CME: $INX)

Since the 1990s and the launch of SPY, the market has had clearly defined bull and bear cycles where the MACD lines oscillate above and below the zero line – offering unambiguous triggers as they mirror the histogram. The market cycles were not always so clear cut in the past and the MACD lines sometimes crossed over for a re-entry signal without falling below the zero line first. This type of signal tends to occur during trading ranges or on the final leg of a bull market.

FIGURE 40: DOW JONES INDUSTRIAL AVERAGE ($INDU) AND S&P 500°
($INX) OVERLAY 1967-1977

A longer look-back period would be helpful to examine this type of signal in more detail. If we apply the same MACD-H settings to a monthly chart of the Dow Jones Industrial Average^{SM} (INDU) back to January 1927 (just before the Wall Street Crash) and we overlay the INDU and INX charts, we notice the Dow tracks the S&P over the long term and both indices tend to give signals within a few months of each other.

On the Dow, there were six additional 'above-the-line' signals between 1927 and 1967, and the message is the same. This type of signal is more reminiscent of the market cycles prior to the 1990s and tends to occur in trading ranges.

Trading the strategy in 'real life'

As we saw in the **Three Styles** chapter, a monthly trend-following strategy lags the market. Our entries will nearly always occur after the improving economic situation is well known and we might feel like we are missing out. Likewise, our exits will come after the market has started pulling back or even entered a fully-fledged bear market.

During these times, we will be edging to get out of our position and act before we get a signal.

Frequently, the news narrative doing the rounds will be telling the complete opposite story to the MACD-H indicator. When we get a signal to exit, the economy might be booming and the market is once again 'making a new high.' On the other hand, when we get a signal to enter, some high-profile company might have gone bankrupt and shocked everyone.

Commentators like to identify a defining moment which changed the market, but it's more likely things have already changed under the surface and the high-profile event is the final straw, the excuse for everyone to accept the obvious. Every trigger is accompanied by an event which never happened previously, but the market's response is the same. Remember, we are trading the market's response to events, not the events themselves – the events are almost irrelevant.

Frequently the strategy gets close to triggering us out of the position, but the market reverses and carries on as before. This happens because the initial impact of the event is quickly forgotten, and people revert to the underlying mood of greed which is driving the market. We have to hang in there, because the strongest bull markets have regular pullbacks which can give a signal intra-month, but they recover before the month ends and continue upwards.

Patience and discipline

If we are getting close to the end of the month and the strategy is already triggering, do we stick doggedly to the rules and wait for the final day, or do we jump the gun?

Once again, this brings us back to the **Two Choices** of trading. If we take a more aggressive approach and act before the MACD-H confirms, we may have to reverse our order a month later. On the other hand, if we wait for two successive signals before acting, we might have to sit through bigger drawdowns before eventually pulling the trigger.

If we are prone to acting before the signal, we might as well adjust the settings and follow those, but how likely are we to stick to the new settings? Rather than interfering with the settings, we can spend the time examining some other indicators which will give us a hint of where the market might be headed.

Ten-period exponential moving average, calculated from the close (10EMAC)

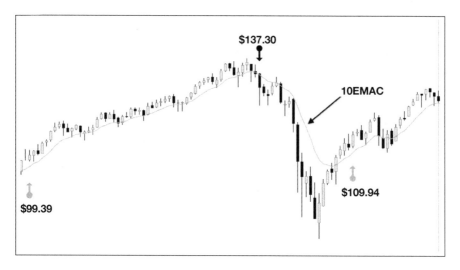

FIGURE 41: CLOSE-UP OF 10EMAC

A 10EMAC line smooths out the volatility of monthly price action and we notice the candles tend to trade above the 10EMAC line on an uptrend and hang below it on a downtrend. When the price closes above or below the 10EMAC, it confirms the trend and will often flag a trend reversal a few months in advance of the MACD-H.

FIGURE 42: USING 10EMAC FOR AN AGGRESSIVE RE-ENTRY

More aggressive traders can take an early signal when at least half a candle has traded on one side of the 10EMAC (depending on whether we are entering or exiting) and the price closes on the same side of the line. However, they need to be careful as the 10EMAC can also dissect the candles when a trend flattens out before resuming. For cautious traders, the trigger to act should always be the histogram's closing relative to the zero line – 10EMAC is an important second opinion, but MACD-H has the final say.

Stocks trading above 50-day moving average

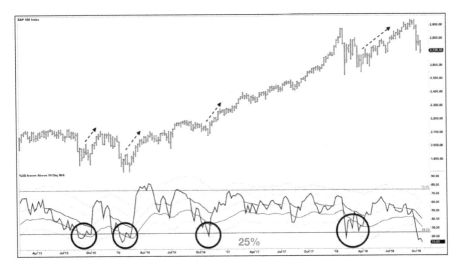

FIGURE 43: WEEKLY CHART OF S&P 500 (CBOE: $SPX.X) AND PERCENTAGE OF U.S. ISSUES TRADING ABOVE 50-DAY MA

On a weekly chart, when we examine the percentage of stocks trading above their 50-day simple moving average, we get another perspective on the market. A reading above 75% indicates overbought conditions. The market often stalls at this point to digest the recent gains before proceeding higher or reversing.

A reading below 25% suggests the market is oversold and a bounce is imminent. The oversold signal is particularly good at identifying selling exhaustion when a pullback (>5% decline from the peak) or a correction (>10% decline from the peak) is ending.

Apart from these horizontal levels, ATR channels applied to the indicator are very useful. The first lower ATR line has a knack of catching the end of pullbacks. When this ATR line is also below the 25% horizontal line, a bounce from this level is a high probability.

Interest rate yield curve[3]

Historically, there is a strong correlation between interest rates and stock prices. In theory, rates go up and stocks go down, and visa versa. Simple logic would suggest the interest rate (yield) on longer-term debt should be higher than short term because the risk of default goes on for longer and investors holding longer term government IOUs (bonds) expect a bigger risk premium. However, on occasions the 'yield curve' becomes inverted which means the short-term rates are higher than the long term. This happens because short-term interest rates are increased to curb inflation in a booming economy, while demand for longer-term debt increases as investors anticipate the bust and load up on long-term bonds, driving those yields down. In the past, this type of pattern in U.S. treasuries occurred prior to a bear market in stocks.

Tidal Strategy versus passive approach

In a 2013 letter to the shareholders of Berkshire Hathaway,[4] Warren Buffett shared the instructions given to the trustee of his will:

> "Put 10% of the cash in short-term government bonds and 90% in a very low-cost S&P 500 index fund. (I suggest Vanguard's.) I believe the trust's long-term results from this policy will be superior to those attained by most investors – whether pension funds, institutions or individuals – who employ high-fee managers."

Over time, a passive 'buy and hold' approach, as suggested by Buffett, will eventually outperform the **Tidal Strategy**, provided the full

---

3   Investopedia, 'Yield Curve Explained' (www.investopedia.com/terms/y/yieldcurve.asp).

4   Warren Buffett, Chairman of Berkshire Hathaway, Letter to Shareholders, 2013 (www.berkshirehathaway.com/letters/2013ltr.pdf).

position is held throughout the entirety of bear markets. This happens because the lagging exit on the **Tidal Strategy** suffers the initial loss after a top and misses out on the initial bounce from a market bottom. The **Tidal Strategy** offers gains over three-, four- and five-year periods. If our horizon is longer, we need to consider an approach like that suggested by Buffett.

Withdrawing cash

The market is not a shrine to capitalism, where we keep putting on gold leaf and never expect to get it back. We need to take our money out at some point and it's imperative we get the timing right. When the market crashes, it radiates out into society and impacts our lives in many ways. If we're not full-time traders, we may lose our jobs or family members might need a helping hand. This strategy puts us into cash to avoid the worst of the bear market, but it also puts cash in our hands (literally) for difficult times.

Geared ETFs

Traders seeking greater returns and willing to embrace more risk might consider a geared ETF such as SSO for this strategy (more about this later). There is currently insufficient historical data to conduct back testing on this ETF but returns from SSO have been more than double those of SPY on the two triggers since 2009.

Conclusion

One of the biggest challenges with this strategy is doing nothing. When a 'risk-on' trigger has been active for a while, especially during an economic boom, we feel we could be putting our money to better use in other assets. On the other hand, when we are in 'risk-off' mode and sitting in cash, we constantly predict the market bottom and are eager to jump back in.

Whenever I share this strategy with beginners, they always ask, '*If this approach to the market is so easy and almost guaranteed to make a profit, why doesn't everyone use it?*' The answer is, like the strategy itself, very simple – most people lack discipline and patience.

THE WILDE
STRATEGY

Introduction

ANOTHER FAVORITE OF mine was inspired by a line from Oscar Wilde:

"We are all in the gutter but some of us are looking at the stars."

This is a discretionary weekly trend-following strategy where we are looking for high-flying stocks that have fallen out of favor and ended up in the gutter.

There can be various reasons for their demise, but once a stock is in the gutter the reason it got there is irrelevant. The company must now adjust to the new reality. Many of the shareholders have been burned and a few diehards have tossed their share certificates in the bottom drawer for the kids.

Life in the gutter

These gutter stocks are like old money families that have fallen on hard times. They have no cash flow, but they often have valuable assets and an air of grandeur about them. They believe their natural home is among the stars and that gives them a twinkle in the eye. Their name is still well known, so building a brand name is not required. Admittedly, they probably have a bad reputation by now, but there is no such thing as bad publicity.

The gutter can be a comfortable place, once you grow accustomed to the smell and the neighbors. Getting out will require a lot of effort. As the management (what's left of them) go about the job of restructuring, the share price finds a bottom and begins to form a base. Over time the price settles into a trading range as resistance and support zones define the width of the gutter.

This process of rattling up and down will make or break the firm, and there are only three ways out. They will go bankrupt and expire, they will restructure and recover, or they will be taken over. New money likes to marry old money to gain respectability and social mobility, so gutter stocks are very attractive takeover targets. In the meantime, there will be attempts to break out of the trading range – but these will usually fail to hold, and the price will fall back into the grime. We are not out yet!

Moving up in the world

These attempted breakout moves can be sudden and violent. The share price can jump higher in a very short time as it leaps out of the gutter, but we must avoid the temptation to buy on these false upside breakouts. We should wait until the upper resistance level of the trading range is broken from below and it is subsequently tested from above and holds as support. This should form the first higher low of a new trend and the recovery has officially begun. We are out of the gutter and heading for the stars.

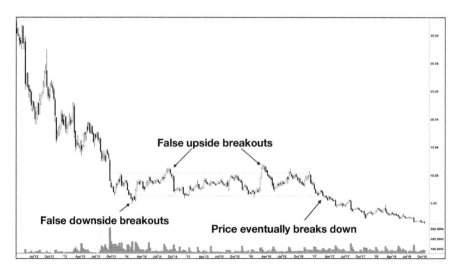

FIGURE 44: WEEKLY CHART OF J.C. PENNY (NYSE: JCP) SHOWING FALSE UPSIDE BREAKOUTS BEFORE EVENTUALLY BREAKING DOWN

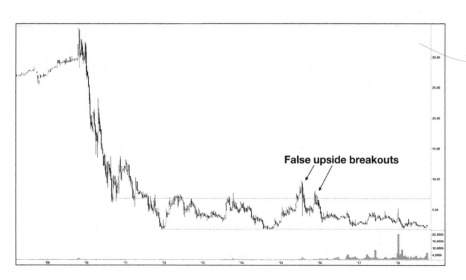

FIGURE 45: WEEKLY CHART OF FLUENT (NASDAQ: FLNT) SHOWING FALSE UPSIDE BREAKOUTS BEFORE RETURNING TO THE GUTTER

FIGURE 46: WEEKLY CHART OF WENDY'S (NASDAQ: WEN) SHOWING CONFIRMED BREAKOUT AND NEW UPTREND

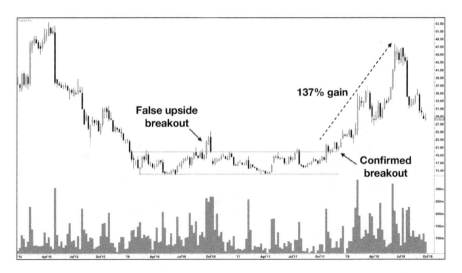

FIGURE 47: WEEKLY CHART OF TWITTER (NYSE: TWTR) SHOWING CONFIRMED BREAKOUT AND NEW UPTREND

The signal to enter this one is not as straightforward as the Tidal Strategy, because our primary indicator is the upper resistance zone of the gutter holding as support after a breakout, and these levels can be spongy at the best of times. In addition, the price action might not be in the form of a clear washout of the zone in a single week or two;

it could be a messy multi-bar washout. For this reason, discretionary traders will prefer this strategy.

This trade is only valid if the share price survives the first serious assault by the grumpy bears and they fail to drive the price back into the gutter. In practice, this means we will miss the first part of the move, as we wait for the stock to form its first higher low above the support/resistance zone.

Earnings

With the **Wilde Strategy,** we are trying to get into a long-term trend which develops as the firm recovers, so we will manage the new trend (if it develops) on a weekly chart with a trailing stop. We will also be holding the stock through earnings, so we can reduce our position before announcements if we practice a more cautious trading style.

FIGURE 48: LUMBER LIQUIDATORS (NYSE: LL) BROKE OUT OF THE GUTTER BUT DISAPPOINTING EARNINGS DROVE IT BACK DOWN

These earnings announcements will now take on greater significance for shareholders and traders, because the recent run-up in price will be based on high expectations and investors will be looking for these to translate into actual profits. If this is not the case, the resulting disappointment will smash the stock down and maybe even back into the gutter.

Scanning for stocks

We can find Wilde trades in a few ways. Fundamentals are a great place to begin. Perhaps there are ongoing internal issues in a firm or a string of unflattering news stories have hit the headlines recently. A declining industry which needs to reinvent itself in order to survive is another possibility – basically anything which indicates a firm is in trouble.

These searches will throw up a list of candidates which are still in a downtrend, but if the capitalization, margin and liquidity figures are reasonable, they have a chance of survival and we should put them on our **Wilde watchlist**.

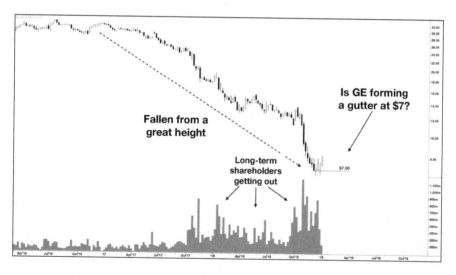

FIGURE 49: WEEKLY CHART OF GENERAL ELECTRIC (NYSE: GE). IS IT STARTING TO FORM A GUTTER AT $7? THIS GOES ON THE WATCHLIST FOR 2019

From a technical perspective, since we are looking for stocks which have fallen from a great height and bottomed out, we can scan for short-term moving averages which have crossed above longer-term moving averages. Another good scan for Wilde trades is to look for stocks which are trading at a new high price for the first time in a year after making multiple bottoms. This will often catch stocks as they break through the upper level of the gutter after bouncing around inside.

In plain view

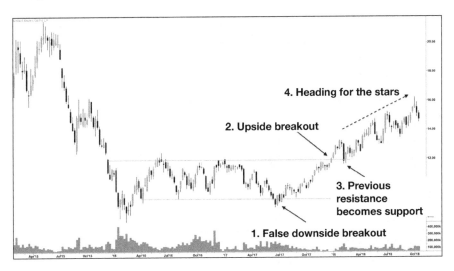

FIGURE 50: WEEKLY CHART OF UNITED STATES OIL FUND (NYSE: USO) SHOWING BREAKOUT PATTERN AND NEW WEEKLY TREND

Sometimes, we don't have to scan a bunch of stocks for Wilde trades as they happen in plain view on main indices or commodities. For example, in June 2017, the United States Oil Fund ETF offered a beautiful Wilde trade as it bounced off the lower gutter and broke through the upper level seven months later. This level held as support, confirming a Wilde trade in oil was on. By October 2018, USO had gained over 87% from the June low.

Discussion

Enormous patience is required if a Wilde trade is to be successful. Many months can pass before the height of the gutter is clearly defined. In the meantime, minor (short-term) resistance and support levels can crystalize inside the gutter. We need to sit patiently watching all of this unfolding, but it's worth the wait. If these stocks break out, the follow up move can be prolonged and incredibly profitable.

If we have difficulty staying in a Wilde trade after it breaks out, a good tip is to stay away from the news and blank out the price bars on the chart, so only the trailing stop is visible.

The challenge with this one is finding the stocks in the first place and then having the patience to monitor our watchlist. Many of the candidates will never recover and we just have to let them go. In addition, stocks can form gutter channels at different price levels over the years and we might only catch one of them.

For those we do catch, trading them is very straightforward: if we prefer a lag-orientated approach to trailing stops we use the -1ATR channel on a weekly chart and if whipsaw is our thing, a stop -1.75ATR below the lowest point of the previous week's price bar is more appropriate.

THE HELP-UP
STRATEGY

Introduction

THE HELP-UP STRATEGY is designed to catch a short-term market bounce and following uptrend based on stocks making new highs and new lows for the past month. There is no scanning for stocks, and as a mechanical strategy it offers clear entry and exit signals. It's suitable for a part-time trader who can check the market every afternoon before the close.

The inspiration for this strategy came from SpikeTrade.com, where Alex and Kerry have worked with new high–new low data on the U.S. markets for over 12 years. Their website was named after the spike that occurs in the data when a pullback or correction is ending, and a potential market bounce is unfolding.

New high–new low (NHNL)

This is considered a 'market breadth' indicator because it measures the range of the stock market by counting the number of stocks making (or repeating) a new high price and the number making (or repeating) a new low, for a given look-back period. This is a comprehensive analysis of the market because it takes every ticker into account regardless of market capitalization.

The guys at SpikeTrade developed various indicators to analyze NHNL data and established levels which flag a bounce on different time frames for the U.S. markets. I was so impressed with their results, I explored NHNL in greater detail. I especially wanted to find signal levels for other large international exchanges. But I soon realized I needed a multi-lingual indicator as each market speaks its own language and has a different number of listed stocks.[1]

HELP indicators

My solution was a suite of technical indicators based on new highs exceeding new lows expressed as a percentage of all stocks being monitored or 'highs exceeding lows per cent' (HELP). These indicators can be based on all stocks trading on an exchange or components of an index or sector. They can also be applied to index weightings or created from a composite of different NHNL analysis. Best of all, they work on all time frames and in all large stock markets.

HELP indicators can also be used as a source of long and short trading signals, especially when divergences between an index and HELP indicators emerge. In summary, I believe HELP indicators are the most reliable and accurate leading market indicators available to traders.

---

[1]   According to the World Federation of Exchanges, the number of listed firms varies considerably from one exchange to another. For example, in July 2018 the BES India Limited (Bombay Stock Exchange) had the highest number of listed firms at 5,080, but only one of those was a foreign firm. At the other end of the spectrum, the Beirut Stock Exchange has just ten listed firms.

The three channels

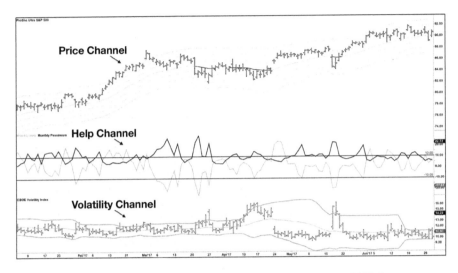

FIGURE 51: HELP-UP STRATEGY, SHOWING THREE CHANNELS

In this strategy, we will use two basic HELP indicators for a daily swing trade on the long side, which incorporates elements of trend following. NHNL data for the U.S. markets is readily available, so this example will be based on the AMEX, NYSE and NASDAQ exchanges.[2]

We plot three channels horizontally on a daily chart, as follows:

1. At the top, we plot a 'price channel' with bars or candles and ATR Channels.

2. In the middle, we create a 'help channel' from NHNL data.

3. Below that, we plot a 'volatility channel'.

Each of these channels examines the market from a different perspective and we get two signals from each. When all six signals concur, we make the trade.

---

2   Excluding exchange-traded funds, warrant stocks, preferred securities, closed end funds, unit investment trusts, non-Standard Industrial Classification stocks, OTC-BB and other OTC stocks.

Let's take a closer look at the three channels:

1. Price channel

To trade this strategy, we need an instrument which tracks the US market closely, while also providing a measure of security and liquidity. eMini S&P 500 futures are suited to this strategy, but geared ETFs are more accessible to part-timers, so we will use one of those.

The ProShares Ultra S&P500® ETF (NYSE: SSO)[3] has net assets of $2.04bn and was launched on 19 June 2006. Apart from holding the components of the S&P 500, it also holds swap contracts and eMinis to achieve a 2× gearing. Their UltraPro S&P500® ETF (NYSE: UPRO) started trading on 23 June 2009 and currently has net assets of $1.07bn and a 3× gearing.

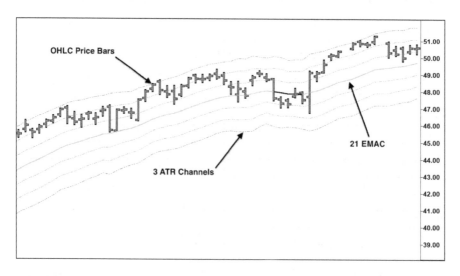

FIGURE 52: PRICE CHANNEL WITH ATR CHANNELS AND OHLC BARS

We should choose the level of gearing and liquidity we are comfortable with, and plot the corresponding ETF on a daily chart using OHLC bars. Over that, we plot three ATR channels with a 21-day EMAC.

---

3   ProShares Website, 31 December 2018. SSO: www.proshares.com/funds/sso. html. UPRO: www.proshares.com/funds/upro.html.

A 20EMAC was the setting used by the 'Turtles', but the difference in profitability between 20EMAC and 21EMAC settings is negligible for the purpose of this strategy.

2. *Help channel*

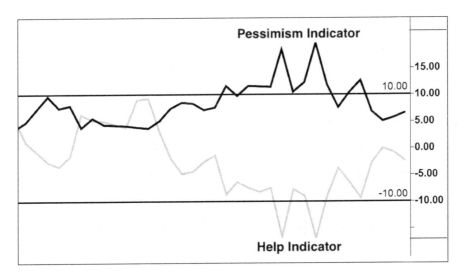

FIGURE 53: CLOSE-UP OF THE HELP CHANNEL

The most popular time period for NHNL analysis is 52 weeks, but this is a daily swing trade, so a one-month window using 20 days is more appropriate. The help channel is created by drawing two horizontal lines at 10% and -10%, and these will provide the trading signals. Next, we plot two indicators using monthly NHNL data:

(a) **Help indicator:** Here, we count the number of stocks making or repeating a new 20-day high and the number making a new 20-day low. We subtract the lows from the highs and plot the result as a percentage of all the stocks we are monitoring.

The help indicator deducts all new lows from all new highs. It considers a stock trading at $850 with a volume of 5,000,000 making a new high, as equal to a stock making a new low at 0.50c with an average volume of 18,000. Because these two stocks cancel each other out in the calculation (one high minus one low), the help indicator considers $4.25bn worth of risk transference as equal to $9,000 worth.

This is the complete opposite perspective to how weighted indices are calculated, because market capitalization is ignored. I believe this help indicator works because most investors and traders also ignore market capitalization when selecting stocks: they go for the story or the price action.

(b) **Pessimism indicator**: This is the second indicator in the help channel and it's calculated from stocks making new lows without regard for new highs. We divide the number of new lows by the total number of stocks and plot the result as a percentage.

3. Volatility channel

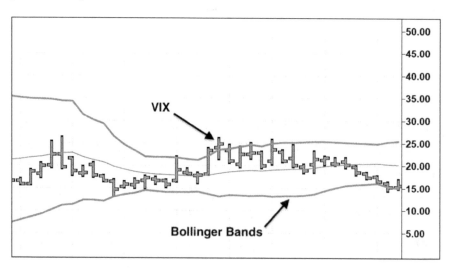

FIGURE 54: CLOSE-UP OF THE VOLATILITY CHANNEL

Panic indicator: And finally, we plot the Chicago Board Options Exchange Volatility Index (VIX) with OHLC bars and apply a standard 20-period Bollinger Band to it. There are numerous methods used by traders to monitor VIX, but this simple and effective method was generously shared with the members of SpikeTrade by Grant Cooke, an experienced trader from California.

VIX is a measure of implied volatility based on 30-day options pricing. Commonly misinterpreted as 'Wall Street's fear gauge', it's really a gauge of the market cost of volatility – the expectation is implied in the price. We already discussed the importance of volatility in the **Nine Filters** chapter, and we are looking at it from two perspectives in this strategy. The expectation of volatility (implied) is captured with VIX in the volatility channel, and the result of volatility (realized) is expressed in ATRs in the price channel.

The six signals

We need six confirmed signals for a trigger to enter the trade. A handy way to remember them is the following phrase: 'Price Helps Pessimism and Panic.'

1. The pessimism indicator is the primary signal upon which everything else depends and there can be no trade until this indicator flags a signal. It must close above the upper channel line (10%) for at least one day and close back below it again.

This indicator is like a heart monitor to the market bear. When it fluctuates wildly up and down, the bear is active. However, when it suddenly drops back into the help channel and stays there pulsating gently, the bear has fallen into hibernation mode. He will eventually come back to life; but, for now, the bulls are in charge.

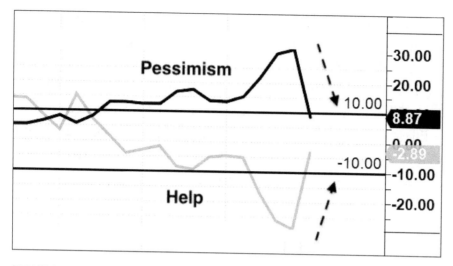

2. When the help indicator closes below the lower help channel line (-10%) for at least one day and closes above it again, we have a help signal.

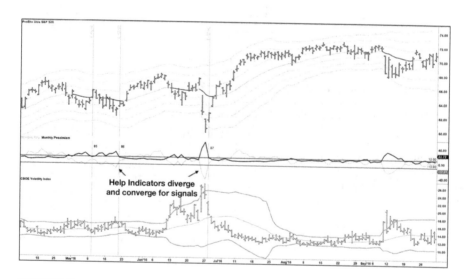

FIGURE 56: DIVERGING AND CONVERGING HELP INDICATORS

In the normal course of events, the two indicators in the help channel zig-zag up and down in a seemingly random fashion. However, when a good trade is setting up, they breach the help channel in opposite directions and converge again in perfect symmetry.

3 & 4. The next two signals are based on **price action** – the importance of which we discussed in the **Ten Tools** chapter. Remember, this strategy is all about a market reversal, so we are looking for the price bars to form a clearly defined 'V'-shaped pattern. We need a clear washout of the past five days' lows, preferably in one or two price bars *and* the price bar must close positive (close higher than open) on the day we take the trade.

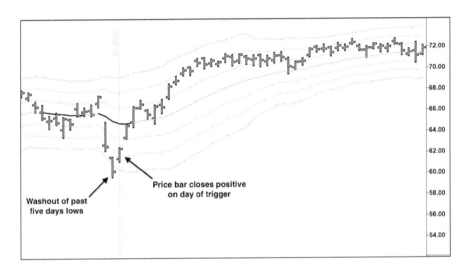

FIGURE 57: CLOSE-UP OF THE PRICE ACTION SIGNAL

5 & 6. The final two signals are related to **panic**. First of all, VIX must pierce its upper Bollinger Band and close back below it *or* close below the mid-line. Secondly, the VIX bar must close negative (close lower than open) regardless of its location in the Bollinger Band.

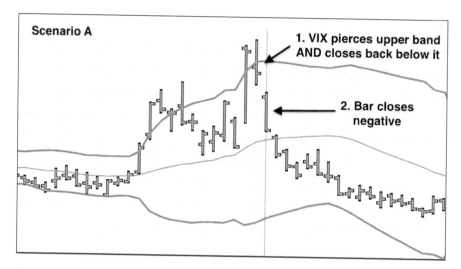

FIGURE 58: SCENARIO A FOR A VIX SIGNAL

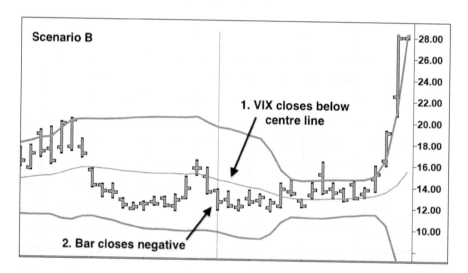

FIGURE 59: SCENARIO B FOR A VIX SIGNAL

As the market alternates between periods of low and high volatility, the Bollinger Bands will expand and contract around the VIX like a bellows. It's often the case that the bands compress so tightly during a period of prolonged low volatility, that the two panic signals occur with just a slight move of the VIX.

Trading the strategy

(a) We enter the position just before the close. NHNL data for the U.S. markets is drawn from approximately 5,000 stocks – all moving independently. A consensus will emerge as the day progresses, so the later we enter the trade, the more informed our decision will be.

This means we often pay the highest price of the day, especially if demand is flooding into the market towards the close. If we decide to wait for the following day to place our trade, in the hope of catching a better entry on a pullback, we can miss the entry totally, especially if the price gaps up at the open.

We place an initial protective stop 0.5ATR below the low of the price bar on the day of the trigger and this 'initial stop' is never moved.

(b) Once we're in the trade, we trail a stop at 1.75ATR below the low point of each previous day's bar. When this moves higher than the initial stop, we switch to the trailing stop.

Our initial stop is tight enough to get us out quickly if the trade doesn't work out, but it also allows us to trade a bigger position size. If the market takes off, our trailing stop is loose enough to catch most of the trend which develops.

Protective stop placement

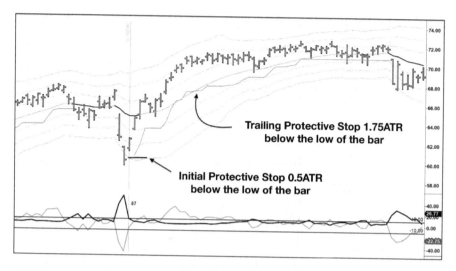

Trailing Protective Stop 1.75ATR
below the low of the bar

Initial Protective Stop 0.5ATR
below the low of the bar

FIGURE 60: PROTECTIVE STOP PLACEMENT

I have used a 21-day look-back period to calculate the volatility-based
protective stops and ATR channels. Some traders use longer ATR
settings for the stops, but I have used the same setting for both as
not everyone has access to charting software to perform separate
calculations. When the same setting is used, the stops can be calculated
visually from the chart.

I've backtested initial stops of 0.5ATR to 0.75ATR, and trailing stops
of 1.5ATR to 2.0ATR below the lows. I've also looked at trailing stops
on the -1ATR line. Of all the possible combinations, the 0.5ATR
initial stop with a -1ATR line trailing stop produced the highest profit.
However, over the entire backtested period (shown below) it produced
only 0.6% more profit than a trailing stop at 1.75ATR below the lows.

When you examine every trade using the two trailing stops, you
realize the -1ATR line stop is more difficult to live with because the
drawdown can be huge on individual trades, but you gradually make
up the loss over the long run when a good trend develops. A stop set at
-1.75ATR below the lows is tighter and has less drawdown on trades,

so it's easier to live with. For this reason, I use the 0.5 and 1.75ATR combination.

Price-reversal pattern

We won't always get a clean 'V' reversal and washout of prices when the trigger occurs. A messy 'gap-and-go' scenario frequently happens when the price compresses for a few days, then gaps up at the open on the day of the trigger and never looks back. In the normal course of events, entering a long position at the closing price of a 'gap-up bar' is not a good idea, but this strategy permits such an entry provided all six signals are present.

Risk management

SPY, SSO and UPRO are highly liquid ETFs and when we apply the first limit of risk (1% maximum position size relative to turnover) to SPY, we notice its current average daily volume of 129.3m and closing price of $249.92 would require a position size of over $323m to exceed 1% daily turnover. For SSO, it would be $2.75m and $2.63m for UPRO.[4]

On the flip side, because of the tight initial stop, it's easy to take on a position which complies with the 1% and 2% limits but exceeds the 20% limit. Due to the liquidity in SSO, traders who are willing to embrace more risk can set aside the 20% rule, but this can mean their entire account is in the ETF if they enter a position during a period of low volatility when the ATR channels are narrow.

Observing the 20% limit will often mean our invested capital is small relative to the size of our account. This happens when volatility is high and the ATR channels are wide, so the initial stop is far below the

---

4   Based on closing prices on 31 December 2018.

entry price in dollar terms. In this situation, when we catch a good market bounce but only have a few bucks in the trade, it can be very frustrating.

Backtested results

No	Entry Date	Price $	Initial Stop	Shares	Exit Date	Price $	Trade % Profit/Loss	Account % Profit/Loss	Year % Profit/Loss
				SSO (Full Position to End)					
					2006				
1	19-Jul-06	34.57	33.36	826	11-Sep-06	36.33	5.09	2.91	2.91
					2007				
2	11-Jan-07	41.79	40.99	1196	27-Feb-07	42.36	1.36	1.36	
3	6-Mar-07	39.83	38.33	667	14-Mar-07	38.33	-3.77	-2.00	
4	15-Mar-07	39.64	38.77	1149	07-Jun-07	46.26	16.70	15.22	
5	11-Jun-07	46.09	45.25	1084	12-Jun-07	45.25	-1.82	-1.82	
6	13-Jun-07	46.35	44.86	671	21-Jun-07	45.87	-1.04	-0.64	
7	2-Jul-07	46.44	45.25	840	24-Jul-07	46.41	-0.06	-0.05	
8	21-Aug-07	41.67	40.23	694	17-Oct-07	45.92	10.20	5.90	
9	26-Oct-07	46.39	44.8	629	01-Nov-07	44.80	-3.43	-2.00	
10	28-Nov-07	41.94	39.57	422	17-Dec-07	41.55	-0.93	-0.33	15.64
					2008				
11	24-Jan-08	35.00	33.33	599	29-Feb-08	33.61	-3.97	-1.66	
12	18-Mar-08	33.74	31.21	395	21-May-08	36.55	8.33	2.22	
13	16-Jun-08	34.79	33.86	1075	18-Jun-08	33.86	-2.67	-2.00	
14	22-Jul-08	30.45	28.57	532	28-Jul-08	28.57	-6.17	-2.00	
15	13-Oct-08	17.75	14.32	292	16-Oct-08	14.32	-19.32	-2.00	-5.44
					2009				
16	24-Nov-08	11.82	10.11	585	12-Jan-09	12.55	6.18	0.85	
17	12-Mar-09	8.90	7.77	885	17-Jun-09	12.77	43.48	6.85	
18	14-Jul-09	12.65	12.16	2041	01-Sep-09	15.38	21.58	11.14	
19	4-Sep-09	15.92	15.2	1389	25-Sep-09	16.75	5.21	2.31	
20	5-Oct-09	16.61	15.93	1471	27-Oct-09	17.33	4.33	2.12	23.27
					2010				
21	5-Nov-09	17.45	16.73	1389	21-Jan-10	19.53	11.92	5.78	
22	2-Feb-10	18.67	17.91	1316	04-Feb-10	17.91	-4.07	-2.00	
23	11-Feb-10	17.88	16.96	1087	16-Apr-10	21.75	21.64	8.41	
24	10-Jun-10	18.00	17.05	1053	24-Jun-10	17.46	-3.00	-1.14	
25	8-Jul-10	17.38	16.65	1370	11-Aug-10	18.01	3.62	1.73	
26	17-Aug-10	18.08	17.57	1961	19-Aug-10	17.57	-2.82	-2.00	
27	1-Sep-10	17.67	16.81	1163	12-Nov-10	21.63	22.41	9.21	
28	18-Nov-10	21.67	21.18	2041	23-Nov-10	21.18	-2.26	-2.00	17.99

No	Entry		Initial		Exit		Trade %	Account %	Year %
	Date	Price $	Stop	Shares	Date	Price $	Profit/Loss	Profit/Loss	Profit/Loss
2011									
29	2-Dec-10	22.58	21.78	1250	20-Jan-11	24.67	9.26	5.23	
30	26-Jan-11	25.47	25.11	1963	28-Jan-11	25.11	-1.41	-1.41	
31	1-Feb-11	25.89	25.10	1266	22-Feb-11	26.39	1.93	1.27	
32	25-Feb-11	26.48	25.85	1587	02-Mar-11	25.83	-2.45	-2.06	
33	21-Mar-11	25.58	24.97	1639	23-Mar-11	24.97	-2.38	-2.00	
34	9-May-11	27.45	26.87	1724	16-May-11	26.87	-2.11	-2.00	6% Limit
35	18-May-11	27.27	26.44	1205	23-May-11	26.31	-3.52	Not Taken	
36	26-May-11	26.70	25.93	1299	02-Jun-11	26.00	-2.62	Not Taken	
37	14-Jun-11	25.20	24.71	1984	15-Jun-11	24.71	-1.94	Not Taken	
38	21-Jun-11	25.47	24.68	1266	23-Jun-11	24.57	-3.53	-2.28	
39	27-Jun-11	24.84	24.05	1266	11-Jul-11	26.49	6.64	4.18	
40	15-Aug-11	21.68	20.49	840	18-Aug-11	20.21	-6.78	-2.47	
41	7-Sep-11	21.40	20.10	769	09-Sep-11	20.10	-6.07	-2.00	
42	13-Sep-11	20.48	19.40	926	22-Sep-11	19.06	-6.93	-2.63	6% Limit
43	5-Oct-11	19.38	17.87	662	01-Nov-11	21.90	13.00	Not Taken	-6.19
2012									
44	20-Dec-11	22.59	21.55	962	06-Mar-12	26.74	18.37	7.98	
45	8-Mar-12	27.5	26.95	1818	09-Apr-12	28.04	1.96	1.96	
46	12-Apr-12	28.35	27.34	990	23-Apr-12	27.34	-3.56	-2.00	
47	6-Jun-12	25.48	24.33	870	25-Jun-12	25.54	0.24	0.10	
48	27-Jul-12	28.25	27.07	847	02-Aug-12	27.07	-4.18	-2.00	
49	3-Aug-12	28.49	27.80	1449	25-Sep-12	30.66	7.62	6.29	
50	19-Nov-12	28.43	27.55	1136	27-Dec-12	29.60	4.12	2.66	15.00
2013									
51	2-Jan-13	31.65	30.77	1136	21-Feb-13	33.57	6.07	4.36	
52	22-Feb-13	34.14	33.4	1351	25-Feb-13	33.40	-2.17	-2.00	
53	27-Feb-13	34.13	32.88	800	05-Apr-13	35.29	3.40	1.86	
54	9-Apr-13	36.58	35.92	1366	15-Apr-13	36.29	-0.79	-0.79	
55	23-Apr-13	37.01	35.85	862	23-May-13	39.99	8.05	5.14	
56	7-Jun-13	40.21	38.99	820	12-Jun-13	38.99	-3.03	-2.00	
57	26-Jun-13	38.26	37.29	1031	15-Aug-13	41.72	9.04	7.13	
58	22-Aug-13	41.01	40.11	1111	27-Aug-13	40.11	-2.19	-2.00	

No	Entry Date	Price $	Initial Stop	Shares	Exit Date	Price $	Trade % Profit/Loss	Account % Profit/Loss	Year % Profit/Loss
59	4-Sep-13	40.83	39.66	855	25-Sep-13	42.90	5.07	3.54	
60	10-Oct-13	42.77	41.45	758	04-Dec-13	47.57	11.22	7.27	22.51
					2014				
61	18-Dec-13	49.12	46.4	368	13-Jan-14	49.63	1.04	0.38	
62	6-Feb-14	47.12	45.61	662	13-Mar-14	51.14	8.53	5.32	
63	31-Mar-14	52.65	51.84	949	07-Apr-14	51.84	-1.54	-1.54	
64	9-Apr-14	52.66	51.00	602	10-Apr-14	51.00	-3.15	-2.00	
65	16-Apr-14	52.03	50.65	725	15-May-14	52.53	0.96	0.72	
66	19-May-14	53.47	52.34	885	12-Jun-14	55.90	4.54	4.30	
67	13-Aug-14	57.22	56.15	935	23-Sep-14	59.57	4.11	4.39	
68	3-Oct-14	58.54	57.15	719	07-Oct-14	57.15	-2.37	-2.00	
69	20-Oct-14	54.78	52.63	465	09-Dec-14	63.00	15.01	7.65	17.23
					2015				
70	18-Dec-14	64.39	61.93	407	02-Jan-15	63.52	-1.35	-0.71	
71	22-Jan-15	64.32	61.22	323	28-Jan-15	61.22	-4.82	-2.00	
72	3-Feb-15	63.44	61.06	420	06-Mar-15	65.12	2.65	1.41	
73	12-Mar-15	64.71	63.03	595	25-Mar-15	65.02	0.48	0.37	
74	27-Mar-15	64.24	63.07	778	30-Apr-15	65.50	1.96	1.96	
75	4-May-15	67.65	66.87	739	05-May-15	66.87	-1.15	-1.15	
76	8-May-15	67.79	66.61	737	12-May-15	66.48	-1.93	-1.93	
77	10-Jul-15	65.43	64.13	764	24-Jul-15	66.15	1.10	1.10	
78	29-Jul-15	67.41	65.87	649	06-Aug-15	65.87	-2.28	-2.00	
79	10-Aug-15	67.26	65.90	735	11-Aug-15	65.90	-2.02	-2.00	
80	27-Aug-15	59.80	56.33	288	01-Sep-15	56.09	-6.20	-2.14	6% Limit
81	5-Oct-15	59.61	57.36	444	12-Nov-15	64.35	7.95	4.21	
82	18-Nov-15	65.72	63.33	418	03-Dec-15	63.76	-2.98	-1.64	-4.51
					2016				
83	21-Jan-16	52.62	50.39	448	08-Feb-16	51.16	-2.77	-1.31	
84	12-Feb-16	52.34	49.7	379	29-Apr-16	64.07	22.41	8.89	
85	10-May-16	65.41	63.76	606	12-May-16	63.76	-2.52	-2.00	
86	20-May-16	63.5	62.53	787	13-Jun-16	65.40	2.99	2.99	
87	28-Jun-16	62.39	60.45	515	26-Aug-16	70.85	13.56	8.72	
88	7-Nov-16	68.64	66.94	588	30-Dec-16	76.13	10.91	8.81	26.10

| No | Entry | | Initial | | Exit | | Trade % | Account % | Year % |
	Date	Price $	Stop	Shares	Date	Price $	Profit/Loss	Profit/Loss	Profit/Loss
					2017				
89	03-Feb-17	79.95	78.85	625	09-Mar-17	84.50	5.69	5.69	
90	15-Mar-17	86.56	84.88	577	21-Mar-17	84.88	-1.94	-1.94	
91	28-Mar-17	84.51	82.40	474	13-Apr-17	82.82	-2.00	-1.60	
92	19-May-17	86.37	85.12	578	27-Jun-17	89.16	3.23	3.23	
93	14-Aug-17	92.68	91.49	539	17-Aug-17	91.49	-1.28	-1.28	
94	22-Aug-17	91.70	89.79	524	25-Oct-17	99.35	8.34	8.01	
95	16-Nov-17	102.10	100.67	489	1-Dec-17	104.01	1.87	1.87	13.97
					2018				
96	12-Feb-18	107.04	102.50	220	1-Mar-18	107.57	0.50	0.23	
97	5-Mar-18	112.41	106.26	160	19-Mar-18	110.98	-1.27	-0.46	
98	5-Apr-18	107.06	104.13	340	6-Apr-18	104.13	-2.74	-1.99	
99	5-Jul-18	112.70	109.97	366	30-Jul-18	117.61	4.36	3.59	
100	16-Aug-18	121.36	119.88	411	4-Oct-18	126.01	3.83	3.82	
101	16-Oct-18	118.19	113.28	203	22-Oct-18	113.28	-4.15	-1.99	
102	1-Nov-18	111.85	107.17	213	14-Nov-18	109.01	-2.54	-1.21	
103	26-Nov-18	106.54	102.93	277	4-Dec-18	108.57	1.91	1.12	3.12
		Average Gain	4.39	%			**Annual Average Gain %**		10.89
		Average Loss	-1.71	%					
			38.95%	RRR					
		Winners	51						
		Losers	48						
		Not Taken	4						

FIGURE 61: SPREADSHEET OF BACKTESTED RESULTS FOR 103 TRIGGERS ON THE HELP STRATEGY (JULY 2006–DECEMBER 2018)

Results on a simulated $50,000 account for SSO, max 2% risk per trade, 20% limit of risk set aside, full position held throughout, dividends not included, no margin.

Every valid trigger was included in the results above, regardless of market conditions or trading skill. It's beneficial to see what would happen if the strategy was traded blindly in all market conditions, so we have the confidence to enter trades knowing what the worst-case scenario looks like.

When a trade was carried over the year end, it was booked in the following year.

Entries are based on the closing price of the day the trigger activated. Our entries on a real account would differ slightly, as we enter about 15 minutes before the close.

When in a position and SSO gapped down at the open and began trading below the protective stop, the opening price was taken as the exit price. Due to the high liquidity, a market order is almost always filled immediately at the open or very close to it.

When two help triggers occurred in succession and the first trade had not been stopped out, the second trigger was ignored. In a real account, aggressive traders may wish to increase their position size when this happens, as it's a very bullish sign.

On two occasions, the price pulled back and traded momentarily at the stop level before reversing and going higher. In a real account, the stop-loss order may not have triggered or the order might have been partially filled depending on its size. However, for the purposes of backtesting, it is assumed both orders executed in full.

The 6% limit of risk kicked in twice in 2011. The first prevented a combined loss of 6.07% on three subsequent triggers, while the second one missed a gain of 3.34%. In 2015, the limit also kicked in, but no Help-Up trigger occurred during the stand aside month, so it had no impact on the results.

Because this is a mechanical strategy which tracks the market, I stand aside for a month after an accumulated loss of 6%, even if it took more than 30 days to accumulate that loss. The 6% rule based on a 30-day rolling month breaks a trader's losing streak, whereas this method sidesteps a market losing streak.

Dividends, trading expenses and inflation

Dividends and trading expenses would influence the results, while inflation and reinvestment of profits would increase the account, but I have maintained the balance at $50,000 throughout for simplicity. Like the Tidal Strategy, dividends received should be more than enough to cover the trading expenses and would add considerably to the returns over the long run. Neither were included in the results shown above.

Analysis of the results

The **Help-Up Strategy** is like a harp and triggers are the strings. It has given an average annual return of 10.89% on the simulated account. However, the results should be seen as the worst-case scenario, the sound produced when the triggers are mechanically followed by anyone. In the hands of an experienced professional, this strategy will produce sweet and profitable music.

In this block of 103 triggers, 51 were profitable and 48 were loss-making (four were not traded because the 6% limit of risk was exceeded). With a 51.5% 'win rate' and a risk/reward ratio of 1.71/4.39 (38.95%), the strategy meets the requirements of the fifth limit of risk.

The largest profit in a trade was 43.48% in June 2009 (no. 17), but this only increased the account balance by 6.85% because of position sizing. The biggest loss was 19.32% in October 2008 (no. 15) which only resulted in a full 2% loss in the account thanks to robust risk management.

The best year (2009) had the least amount of triggers (5) and they were all profitable. The worst year (2011) had 15 triggers and 11 of those were loss-making, including seven losses in a row. This would appear to confirm the notion that less trading is more profitable.

Of the 99 exits on SSO, five occurred on a gap down below the protective stop and four of those were in 2011. The biggest single loss in the account over the entire backtested period was 2.63% on a gap down on 22 September 2011 – painful, but not the end of the world.

A closer look at the signals

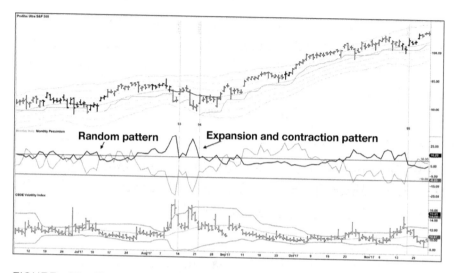

FIGURE 62: EXPANSION AND CONTRACTION PATTERNS IN HELP CHANNEL

When the strategy triggers, the help and pessimism signals are unmistakable. They go outside the help channel and return in a symmetrical 'expansion and contraction' pattern. This is in stark contrast to the higgledy-piggledy patterns which they print out most of the time. It's as if the market barks an order at them and they snap into the correct formation.

A help trigger where all six signals happen on the same day offers the most profitable trades. However, it's also acceptable for three or four signals to occur on one day and the others to fall into place a day or so later. The sequence doesn't matter, provided all the signals are still present on the day we enter.

Most importantly, if we get two signals from the help channel but the other signals fail to line up within five days, the trade is off. On these occasions, we should consider the signals invalid and start again.

The help indicator

The help indicator isn't like volume or MACD-H indicators, where we watch closely for a small tick up or down to reveal something. A good help trigger is like any other good setup, we should be able to see it clearly with our reading glasses off.

We could just as easily shift the help channel to 9% or 11%, either way. This would include or exclude a handful of signals but make little difference in the overall scheme of things. Good help signals are obvious, the lines burst outside the channel and reverse sharply.

The help indicator is like a support/resistance zone, there is a bit of give in it. Let's not forget, this indicator is a measure of shifting imbalance in the market. The stocks we are counting are at the highest or lowest they have been for the past month, we're measuring the monthly peak of euphoria and depression – let's not quibble over half a per cent of emotion!

The pessimism indicator

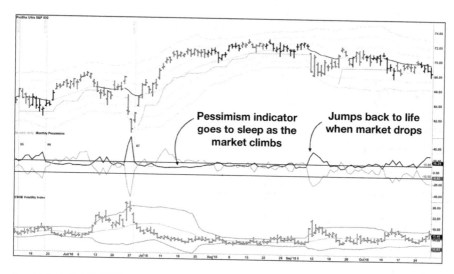

FIGURE 63: FOCUS ON THE PESSIMISM INDICATOR

This has to remain inside the help channel if the trade has any chance of success. False positive signals[5] all share a common trait – the pessimism indicator is unsure of itself and tends to zig-zag on the upper channel line without making a firm decision. In good trades, it shoots outside the channel, drops back in and stays there for long periods as the bear sleeps.

In fact, the pessimism indicator can be used as a market internal indicator in its own right. Simple logic dictates, in order for a market index to continue making new monthly highs, more than 10% of stocks can't also continue to make new monthly lows. The index and indicator can diverge for a short period, but not for long!

---

5   I define a false positive as an occasion where the Help Strategy gave a valid trigger, with all six signals present, but the market bounce was short-lived and the resulting trade incurred a loss or broke even.

Trading in bull markets

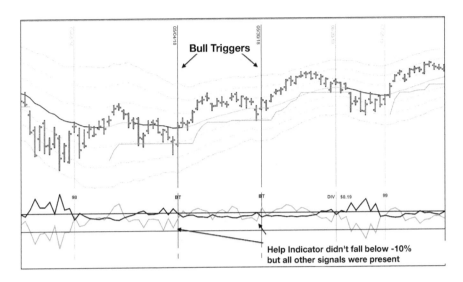

FIGURE 64: BULL TRIGGERS

In a strong bull market, there will be few triggers (because there are few pullbacks) and when they do occur, they happen quickly. On these occasions, the help indicator might not drop below the lower line of the help channel but comes within a whisper of it.

This is when we need to give greed the benefit of the doubt. If the help indicator pulls back briefly, nearly flags a signal, but doesn't and all the other signals line up perfectly (especially the pessimism indicator), more aggressive traders can take the trade, because these 'bull triggers' frequently offer the most profitable opportunities.

For example, on 8 December 2017 a bull trigger gave a profit of 12.6% before it was stopped out on 30 January 2018. The trade also collected a dividend payment of $0.16 per share. Numerous other bull triggers occurred during the backtested period (there were two between triggers 98 and 99, figure 64), but I haven't included any bull triggers in the results.

Trading in bear markets

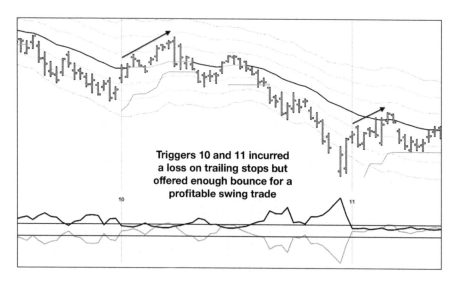

Triggers 10 and 11 incurred
a loss on trailing stops but
offered enough bounce for a
profitable swing trade

FIGURE 65: SWING TRADES IN A BEAR MARKET

In bear markets, we may get a short market bounce, but there will be no following uptrend. In this case, the triggers should be used to catch reaction rallies using daily swing trades. These trades should last a few days and the entire position should be closed out after the initial bounce begins to falter. It's rare for a valid trigger not to offer a profitable counter-trend swing trade in a bear market.

False positives as a market internal indicator

The **Help-Up Strategy** tends to get a cluster of false positive triggers just before a market sell off. For example, in 2011 and 2015 the strategy incurred a series of triggers, but the market didn't bounce. Instead, the market trended sideways just before it dropped.

Following a market bounce and help trigger, eager buyers should flood into the market with demand for shares – this absorbs the available supply at the current price level and drives the market higher. A failure to do this is an indication of some serious negative sentiment under the surface. If there is no follow-through after the initial signal and the pessimism indicator stays above the help channel (>10%) – something is seriously wrong!

Hybrid trades and experience

If our analysis indicates the market is in a transition phase, or we are just not comfortable holding a full position, we can catch the initial bounce with a swing trade and bank some profits by closing half or a third of the position. Then, a trailing stop can be used under the remainder to catch a bullish trend, if it develops.

This hybrid style offers the best of both worlds. By grabbing some profit early on, we get our trade into a break-even position, but we also get the benefit of a trend.

This approach is especially useful following a sharp correction as the low of the initial stab down is frequently retested soon after. However, some of the most profitable trades begin with just one stab down and a 'double bottom' doesn't always occur. One way to address the issue is to reduce our position size on the first trigger after a correction and trade a full position if that low is retested.

The use of discretion in situations like this allows experienced traders to significantly increase the profitability of the strategy. Help-Up constantly provides profitable opportunities – how we leverage them is up to us.

Live trading and follow up

In the **Four Legs** chapter, I wrote "Strategies look great in a small book, but they often crumble when they make it to the big screen." With this in mind, I began to record live videos of this strategy from August 2017 onwards. Trigger no. 94 occurred soon after and gave a profit of 8.34% on the trade and 8.01% on the simulated account. Trigger 103 was the final trade to close in 2018. Trigger 104 occurred on 31 December 2018, but the position was carried into 2019 so it wasn't included in the results above.

At murphytrading.com, I offer a complete education program as a follow up to this book and it includes the videos mentioned above. I continue to trade this strategy in my own account.

The Help-Down Strategy

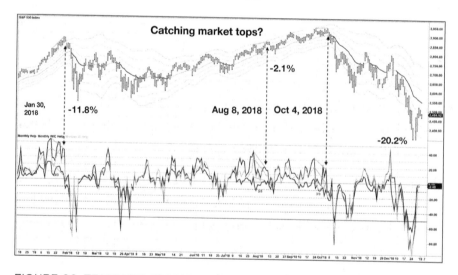

FIGURE 66: TRIGGERS IN 2018 ON THE HELP-DOWN STRATEGY

The Help-Up Strategy is a long-only strategy not designed to produce profits when the market is heading south. For that, I am developing the **Help-Down Strategy** which also uses NHNL data, but from a different perspective. Timing a market pullback is notoriously difficult, not to mention catching a market top, so short strategies are more challenging to develop.

Help-Down is based on divergences between three help indicators and price. So far, results suggest the best triggers have diverging peaks 8–12 days apart. If the long-term results confirm the initial analysis, I plan to merge the strategies and trading them will involve reversing a position.

For example, between triggers no. 95 and no. 96 on the Help-Up Strategy, the Help-Down version triggered three days before the February 2018 correction. On 4 October 2018, when trigger no. 100 on the Help-Up Strategy was about to be stopped out, Help-Down flashed a trigger to short the market. In my real account, I canceled the protective stop on the open Help-Up trade and reversed the position. Take a look at the right edge of the chart in figure 66 to see what happened next!

THE
BEGINNING

T O EXTRACT DIAMONDS from a mine, thousands of tons of dirt and rock have to be processed. It's a huge operation which requires excavators, dump trucks, conveyors and screening plants. Typically, the mine is located in the middle of nowhere and the local town is full of conmen.

The financial markets are also a diamond mine. But, how many of us are prepared to work in such a hostile environment, especially when most of us only have a sieve and shovel?

Trading involves work and effort. We have to dig through tons of data and charts and often our only reward is a few specks of profit. But, it's worth the hassle, because every so often a huge shiny gem appears on our shovel and we just have to pick it up. What's more, the market mine is unique because the seam of rough diamonds never runs out.

When you trade the markets, there is no guarantee you'll get richer. However, in my experience, and based on the honest anecdotal experience of other professional traders, if you work at it and stay at it, you will make money.

How much you make, will depend on what you picked up from these pages.

I wish you well!

THE
ACKNOWLEDGEMENTS

D R. ALEXANDER ELDER encouraged me to write and made the introduction which led to the publication of this book – for that I will always be grateful. The chapters on risk management, trading methods and records were strongly influenced by Alex's work.

The chapters on technical analysis, stock screening and trading tools are based on instructions and advice I received from Kerry Lovvorn. He impressed upon me the importance of analyzing factual data to interpret the market correctly, I am most thankful for that.

One Valentine's Day, I decided to get something special for the love of my life – so I bought myself a subscription to Spiketrade.com. This online community, where serious traders compete for prizes and prestige in a friendly and helpful atmosphere, has been a treasure trove of insights and advice; my thanks to the members.

While I was pounding the keys, my agent in New York, Ted Bonanno, was pounding the pavement. Carol Kayne proofread the first draft of the manuscript and Christopher Parker at Harriman House edited the wheat from the chaff and oversaw the cover design and page layout, before Liz Bourne proofread the final book. I thank them all for their invaluable assistance in bringing this project to life.

Anne Sheehan and Maurice Cremin reviewed the Six Edges chapter and reminded me of the importance of motivation in everything we do. I also thank the folks at Dzogchen Beara in West Cork who are living proof lotus flowers grow on rocky cliffs too.

Born during the Wall Street Crash, my mother Nora is living proof that life defaults to the upside. She taught me all about support and resistance. I am grateful for everything she has done over the years, but especially the cups of tea as I wrote.

My father, Matt, had many sayings, including, "'Tis all in the mind." Twenty years later, having spent a month on top of a mountain in France, I realized he was right. His pragmatism and spirit for adventure lives on in these pages.

When not delivering babies, my daughter Carmen helped me backtest strategies and my son Ben provided a welcome sporting distraction on numerous occasions. I am grateful to them both.

Last on the list, but foremost in my thoughts, I thank my wife Siobhán 'Curly' Hegarty. Sadly, she passed away in July 2018 not long after the final draft of this book was sent to the publishers. Without her patience and understanding it would not have been possible. This book is dedicated to Siobhán.

THE AUTHOR

IAN MURPHY IS a successful private trader, trading his own account using trend-following, swing-trading and day-trading strategies. He has studied various facets of trading with a number of experienced traders, including psychology and trading methods with Dr. Alexander Elder. He has also worked closely on technical analysis and trading strategies with Kerry Lovvorn.

Throughout his trading career, Ian has maintained detailed records and a diary documenting the highs and lows of his trading experiences. Over time, he identified the most important aspects of the journey as he began to interact with other traders. The lessons learned have been brought together in his new book, *Way of the Trader*.

Based in Ireland, after college Ian Murphy trained in electronics before travelling in Europe, North Africa and Central America. He returned to Ireland to work in the metal recycling industry, eventually specializing in precious metals. This brought him into contact with the financial markets and he has been an active trader ever since.

murphytrading.com

THE INDEX

CPSIA information can be obtained
at www.ICGtesting.com
Printed in the USA
BVHW042303280319
543998BV00002B/3/P